The Secon| ... irl
Sally's

CH00797236

Sally George

Based on the diaries of Sally George

Acknowledgements: Peter Arthur for enhancing the photographs. The 'old girls' from the 'John Mansfield 1960 to 1970' Facebook page who gave me all the interesting and amusing quotes from their memories of the school. Vicky for the wonderful photograph, with all the names of Class 1A(2).

Quotes and spellings are written as in the original diary.

John Mansfield Secondary Modern School for Girls, Western Avenue, Dogsthorpe, Peterborough in 2007 shortly before demolition

Front cover photo: The Pebbles Holiday Flats, Hunstanton, 1969
Back cover photo: Class 1A(2) John Mansfield School, 1963/64.

Introduction

My best friend Brenda, who I first met when we were 4, gave me a diary for my 14th birthday on the 12th January 1967 and I have recorded each day of my life ever since! I lived in the village of Eye, 3 miles from Peterborough in a bungalow, 19 The Crescent, with my parents, younger brother Ian, Topsy the dog, Sandy the cat, Snowy the rabbit and Horace the goldfish. After leaving the village primary school, in July 1964, I cycled the 3 miles to John Mansfield Secondary Modern School for Girls in Dogsthorpe, from September 1964, with 2 other girls, Ann Foster, who was my age and Lesley Pycroft who was one year older. The other children in the village caught the school bus to a secondary school in Glinton called Arthur Mellows Village College (fondly nicknamed 'Aunty Mary's Village Cowshed'). My brother attended this school and did very well, graduating in Bristol with an Art and Design degree. I was into the fashion and music of the time which was Twiggy, mini skirts and short lived paper clothing and I was mad about 'The Monkees', a pop group and American TV series which became a precursor to 'Friends' in the 90s. Television was still black and white and there were not many programmes in day time. I remember sitting on the floor watching the 'test card' waiting for 'Watch With Mother' to start. As for the telephone, on average, only one household in every street had a one and the installation of our first phone was paid for by the company my father worked for, enabling him to be 'called out' should any problems arise on the cleaning and maintenance at Perkins Engines This was placed in the unheated hall on a three legged telephone table. By the side was a money box for us to contribute to any personal calls we made. I only remember it to be stuffed with I.O.U. notes. We had a party line which meant we shared it and rather than being intrigued by other people's conversations, it was more of an annoyance. We had a square kitchen/dining room warmed up by the electric cooker and a paraffin heater and a front room (known as 'the room') which had a coal fire, where we would go every evening to watch TV. In there was a fold down table, in the bay window, which was used on Sundays. The car was a novelty and friends and family would go out for a drive and call round, unannounced as there was no phone, in the evenings and at weekends.

Both world wars influenced who I am. My grandmother, Laurina May Fletcher from the Lincolnshire fens would not have met my grandfather Charles Crockett from the East end of London if her brother Oliver hadn't died during WW1 out in Burma. Charles brought Oliver's belongings to the Fletcher family home, Broadgate House, Whaplode Drove. My great grandfather Jabez Fletcher was from an agricultural labourer family in Coates, had worked as a policeman for a while and then secured a loan for a house and land in Whaplode Drove. He grew opium poppies to send by train to London for the drug Laudanum and hired out threshing machines, the forerunner of combine harvesters. My mother Rosemary Crockett would not have met my father, Derrick McDonald, from Blairgowrie, Perthshire if he had not joined the Royal Navy towards the end of WW2. He was sent from the mountains of Scotland to the flat marsh lands of Holbeach bombing range around The Wash. He maintains that he spent a lot of time with his mates searching for King John's treasure in that area. Every Saturday night a lorry load of servicemen, known as the 'passion wagon' would meet with the local girls at the nearest market town of Spalding. On one particular night my father was nominated to be the driver and because of this duty was slowly savouring the one pint of beer he was allowed. My mother had been given a gin and orange but didn't like it, so on passing by my father's table she poured it in his beer and said 'Have a drink on me sailor'! As they say, reader, she married him!

I was born in the village of Eye, which is 3 miles from Peterborough and 10 miles from Whaplode Drove. My grandmother Laurina had been widowed in 1946 after a lonely life due to my grandfather Charles, who was a wireless officer in the Merchant Navy, being at sea most of their married life . At the same time, within days, William (Bill) Gates a boot and shoe retailer and repairer in the High Street, Eye lost his lovely wife Dorothy (known as Dean) who had died in her sleep on Valentine's Day suddenly without any apparent illness. They had no children and he was devastated. These two lonely people met up through 'whist drives' organised by two ladies with the delightful names of Mabel Noble and Hetty Pretty! So my grandmother married Bill and moved to Eye to help run the shoe shop business and her 2 children, my mother Rosemary and her brother Colin moved in too. My parents were married at Eye church in 1950 and on 12th January 1953 I was born at the terraced house of Mrs. Bland, the midwife, situated next door to the Spade and Shovel pub on the High Street and across the road from the shoe shop. If we needed a Doctor then the surgery was on certain days in the front room of a terraced house, in the High Street. I remember my brother hiding behind the sofa in there to escape a vaccination injection. Dr. Geogehan and Dr. Gallagher were the names I remember and they would have several villages to drive to.

My parents had lived in 'rooms' down Fletton Avenue in Peterborough when they were first married as there was a shortage of accommodation after the war. They did hear of a 'condemned cottage' available in Crowland and moved into this 'one up, one down' terraced house down an alley way called 'Thames Tunnel', thus called because someone had been to London and stolen a sign! Apparently everyone commented on how homely my mother had made this poor dwelling by placing coco matting on the floor. There were paraffin lamps on the wall for light, a black range in the fireplace for cooking, a standpipe down the alley for water and an earth closet toilet outside. The stairs were in a cupboard and curved up to the next floor. There were rats between the floors so we acquired a big black cat, whom my Uncle named 'Sambo' but he was scared! This was my first home as a baby! After a year or two, another house became available in East Street where the Library now stands. The house had all amenities and was next door to Greens the bakery. My brother Ian Charles was born here in 1956 and my first memory is of being taken by the hand, up the stairs to see my baby brother. I couldn't work out why my mother was in bed during the day with her nightie on. Also the only word I knew similar to Ian was 'iron' so thought it was a strange name! My other memories were playing in the tin bath, from the hook on the back of the door, as a paddling pool outside and next door Philip Green would teach me how to make mud pies! I also had my biker friends whose names I think were Marilyn and Jacqueline. (My mum always put a bow in my hair). Crowland Abbey is in the background of this photo and the house on the left has since been demolished.

My parents names were on the 3 year waiting list for a Council house. My grandmother was shamed by her customers at letting this be so and a 'deposit' was loaned to my parents in order that they could have a two bedroomed bungalow built in Eye. I still remember the red note book which had an account in of the payments from dad's pay packet each week. He worked at Perkins Engines as a tool cutter grinder. He worked long hours from 7.30 a.m. to 8.30 p.m. plus weekends, apart from when he worked the night shift. A big Council estate was being built behind Back Lane in Eye and so our bungalow was sandwiched between about half a dozen new private houses and old people's bungalows. I remember going out for country lane walks with my mum and brother down Crowland Road on to Green Road, White Post Road and back over Hodney Bridge to the High Street. My mum would wear a pretty Sunday best summer dress, 1950s style which became known as her 'moo moo' dress as we always saw a field of cows on the route.

My brother and I started school in the infants on Eyebury Road but then for juniors the old Victorian buildings on the Crowland Road were used until about 1961 when a new junior school building was added to the existing infants on the Eyebury Road site. The old Victorian school had two classrooms in a building one side of the road, and, in what is now the library across the road, probably had about 3 or 4 rooms. I liked to sit near the wall where the hot water pipes ran so that I could warm my feet on these. I was told off by mum because I would get chilblains. At primary school I remember one class had 48 pupils, and there were no teaching assistants back then. I've since heard reports of 52 children per class as not being unusual. We only had one class per year and only the top 3 children would pass the 11-plus, so I wasn't one of them. We were able to play out in the street all day, such games as 'Queenie, Queenie, who's got the ball?' and 'What's the time Mr. Wolf?'. Our cat would sleep in the middle of the road all day and not be disturbed. The photo shows the new junior school on Eyebury Road with the previously built infant school at the back.

Secondary education for the village was a school bus trip to Arthur Mellows Village College in Glinton about 13 miles away. Alternatively, 3 miles away was Eastholm Girls School, Reeves Way, Eastfield, Peterborough or John Mansfield Secondary Modern School for Girls, Western Avenue, Dogsthorpe, Peterborough. Perhaps my parents thought I wouldn't survive the bus journey each day to Glinton with the rest of the children from Eye, so I cycled to John Mansfield school with two other girls, Ann Foster in my year and Lesley Pycroft who was a year older. There were 5 classes in each year. I don't know of any other village children who did this, or went to another school, apart from one girl who was sent to Westwood House a private school in Peterborough and she became a barmaid at the Red Lion. Secondary modern schools which originated in 1944 were designed for the majority of pupils between 11 and 15. Those who achieved the highest scores in the 11-plus, were allowed to go to a selective grammar school which offered education beyond 15. In the Peterborough area we had two grammar schools for boys, Kings and Deacons, and yet only one county grammar school for girls. At John Mansfield school there was a class 4X for those who wished to take C.S.E., (Certificate of Secondary Education) but if you worked hard to attain a Grade A, it was only equivalent to a Grade C in a G.C.E., (General Certificate of Education). I decided to follow in my

mother's footsteps and embarked on a two year commercial course. This was offered at Peterborough Technical College funded by the government rather than by private means as in my parents' day. I would then be qualified to enter into any field that interested me, as office, admin and support work was needed wherever you went.

The school leaving age was 14 for my mother in 1945. She was sent to work in the village post office which conjures up the romantic idea of 'Lark Rise to Candleford' by Flora Thompson but this was far from the truth. Mum was in the background on housework duties but I remember her talking about the switchboard for telephone calls as the operator had to contact each area exchange to put a call through to a house phone. When her father arrived home from the Navy he paid for my mother to go on a commercial course to learn shorthand, typing, office practice and book-keeping at Bean's Commercial School in Peterborough Cathedral Precincts. She completed most of the course but when her father died her mother wasn't prepared to keep paying the fees for an education which was wasted on a girl, who was destined to become a wife and mother! The skills learned enabled my mother to have a more interesting job other than household duties. She became a bookkeeper for a shoe shop and opticians before she had children and later embarked on office work at Perkins Engines and Peterborough Technical College.

A more modern photograph of 'Peterborough Technical College' as I knew it.

Dramatis Personae taken from the family's 1966 Address Book

Abbott, Mr. & Mrs. E., friends from Perkins Engines where Dad worked as a tool 'cutter grinder', 120 Central Avenue, Dogsthorpe, Peterborough.
Abbott, Mr. E., a friend of parents and he lived with his wife at 120 Central Avenue, Dogsthorpe, Peterborough.
Adams, Claude & Vi, 2nd cousins on the London ancestry, 40 Crown Woods Way, Eltham, London, SE9 2NN.
Adie, C., friend from Perkins Engines, 42 Cathedral Drive, Spalding.
Allen, Hannah (Robert Walker's sister) 2nd cousins on the Scottish/Hull ancestry at 18 Balunie Terrace, Douglas, Dundee. (Hodgson, Lumley, Walker, Allen)
Allen, Hannah, my Dad's 2nd cousin who lived at 18 Balunie Terrace, Douglas, Dundee, Angus, Scotland. (I think her two sons were called Billy and Francis).
Anne W. was probably Anne Walker in my class at school.
Barber, Mrs., deputy headmistress when English lessons were in the Library.
Barron, James was my Dad's Uncle who left home from Glasgow aged 18 to live in New York and never saw his parents again. He did write to them without fail, once a week and his framed photo was always on the mantlepiece. He lived at 35-34 84th Street, Apt. B12, Jackson Heights, N.Y. 11372 and later at 8642 St. James Avenue, Elmhurst, Queens.
Bedford, George, worked at Perkins Engines with my Dad. Lived with wife Margaret and daughter Vicky at 9 Latham Avenue, Orton Longueville, Peterborough.
Bill and Smudge. Friends of Dad's I believe perhaps from Scotland as Bill McFarlane lived with Smudge (probably surname Smith) from Rauceby in Lincolnshire. Bill, years later married so I don't know what happened to 'Smudge'. Around 1967 they lived at 10 Mere Way, Cambridge.

Campbell. Not in the address book so I have no idea. I am not surprised though as I don't know how my Dad would have entertained anyone with that surname after the Massacre at Glencoe in 1692. We even had to 'boo and hiss' when passing the Campbells soup factory on our way home from Hunstanton!
Canham family lived further down The Crescent near the cul-de-sac. I would take baby Mark out in his pram.

Combe, Phyllis, a penfriend from a Penpal Club I joined. Her address was Box 5, Howe, Idaho, 83277, USA.

Cranswick, Mr. was another of Dad's work mates and lived with his wife and daughter Sandra at 29 Oakleigh Drive, Orton Longueville, Peterborough.

Crockett, Colin (Neville Colin Robert) was my Mum's brother. His wife was Sheila, son Graham and daughter Sharon. They lived at 41 Central Square, Stanground, Peterborough.

Crowson, Mr. and Mrs., daughters were Anna and Claire. Friend of my parents and probably worked at Perkins.

Dora, Aunt, distant relative or family friend and surname could be Papworth or Wyllie living at 70 Backgate, Cowbit, Spalding.

Eggleshaw, Ruth and Roy who were friends of my parents and lived in Nottingham. My Dad may have met Roy whilst on training course with the Navy. They lived in Nottingham at 3 Silverdale Road, Old Basford and later at 8 Pygall Avenue, Gotham.

Fletcher, Billy, my Mum's cousin who lived in several places and had several wives, but not all at once!

Forster, Sue a penfriend who lived at Four Winds, 158 Tower Hill, Upholland, Nr. Wigan, Lancs.

Franks, Miss, art teacher at school. She wore an artist's smock undone at the front so it flapped around and was always going for a smoke in the toilets.

Gates, Bill and Laura, my Grandparents who retired from their shoe shop in Eye to live at 11 Briar Way, Peterborough. I cycled to their house to eat my packed lunch as there was no facility for this at school.

Gifford, Carol neighbour from Crowland whose parents ran the fish and chip shop.

Goodall, Christopher was the nephew of Ruth and Roy Eggleshaw who I met when I was 12 and he was 16. He lived at 167 Harwill Crescent, Aspley, Nottingham. One afternoon we sat while he played all his Beatles records for me and I was smitten for the next 4 years until we met again, and the magic had gone!

Gray, Margaret, who lived across the road from us until her mother died and then she moved with her father and brothers to 65 Belsize Avenue, Woodston, Peterborough.

Green, Fred a 2nd cousin of my Mum and his wife Joyce, son John and daughter Sally. They lived at 'Greenways', Holbeach Drove.

Handley, Mrs., our scary P.E. teacher.

Harkin, Miss, French teacher and form mistress in 3A2.

Harrison, Ann and Elizabeth who lived at 164 Central Avenue, Dogsthorpe. Ann was in my class at school and I used to go home with her at lunch time to eat my sandwiches instead of Susan Ruff's house.

Hasty, Chick and Gracie lived at 52 PrioryRoad, Westwood, Peterborough and Chick (Charles) was a work friend of my Dad. Their children were Linda, and twins Colin and Gillian. A friend of theirs called Ann is on the left.

Hazel, George, a work colleague of my Dad from Perkins. They lived at Dogsthorpe and had two daughters Jackie and Sandra. Jackie and her boyfriend Chuck (Charles) from the American Air Base at Alconbury would often come and babysit for my brother and I. At the age of 12, I was one of their 5 bridesmaids when they were married in 1965.

Healey, Roslyn, Jim and son Sean. We would meet this family at the Hasty's house so they became friends of my parents.

Houldershaw, Mr., (Noel?) a work colleague of my Mum from Perkins. I babysat at their house occasionally.

Jones, Simon and Andrew my second cousins who lived at 26 Queens Hill, Newport, Wales with their Mum Doris and Grandmother Lilly Fletcher.

Judge, Freda and Gilbert, family friends from Whaplode Drove who lived at 87 Sallows Road, Peterborough.

Kendle, Jill (Mum's 2nd cousin), her husband John and children Angela and David. They lived at 49 Malvern Road, Gunthorpe.

Lane, Mrs. was the mother of my Aunty Sheila and lived at Eye Green.

Liz and Dave. Dave Langfield was a workmate with Dad and his fiance was Liz Fowler. They married in 1968 and lived at 77 All Saints Road, Peterborough.

Malster, Miss., Geography teacher with beautiful voice for singing in Assembly. She was only 24 and our first form teacher when I started in Class 1A2.

McDonald, Kenneth. Dad's youngest brother (half brother). He lived with my Granddad and Step Grandmother who we called Aunty Hanny at the Swiss cheese shop and post office at Westlands in Blairgowrie.

McDonald, Uncle Angus, Dad's brother and wife Aunty Cathy, daughters Shonagh and Wendy and son Brian lived at 29 Leslie Street, Blairgowrie, Perthshire, Scotland.

McDonald, Uncle Tommy, Dad's brother and wife Aunty Margaret lived at 'Isdell', Golf Course Road, Rosemount, Blairgowrie, Perthshire, Scotland.

McFarlane, see Bill and Smudge.

Michie, Great Aunty Margaret, Dad's Aunt who lived at 4 Barony Park, Alyth, Perthshire, Scotland.

Newborn, Miss. Headmistress of John Mansfield Secondary Modern School for Girls.

Noble, Mabel, a friend of my Grandmother.

Palmer, Helen and Valerie with their parents Jack and Sophie were neighbours in Crowland. They lived in the house attached to the windmill in Crowland.

Parker, Lynda, a friend in my class at school who lived at 143 Eastern Avenue, Dogsthorpe.

Partridge, J.H., Evelyn and Julia, Mum's friends who lived at 29 Avesbury Gardens, Spalding.

Patricia, friend of Mum's from Perkins Engines offices (Purchases Dept.?) surname may have been **Coles** of 26 Eastgate, Peterborough or **Coulson,** 43 Franklyn Crescent, Peterborough.

Petrie, Barbara a friendly girl at Tech College on the same course and she lived at 30 Woodland Lea, Helpston.

Piccaver, Brenda, my best friend. Also her father George, step-mother Maura, brother Eric and half sisters Annette and Caroline. 'Brenda's Mum' Kathleen, lived in a flat on Park Road and worked at the cafe in Broadway called 'Albert's'.

Roberts, Miss, history teacher and for my last school year in 4A she was our form teacher.

Rome, Mrs. who lived in the house opposite and the only one in the street to have a phone. A telegram was the usual urgent message but Mrs. Rome would kindly pass a message on in an emergency.

Ruff, Laurie. Worked with my Dad at Perkins and when I first went to John Mansfield school I would go to his house with his daughter Susan to eat my packed lunch as no provision was made at school other than for school dinners.

Sanford, Lesley, known as 'Lesley S. from my class 3A2.

Scott, Mr. was a newcomer to the school as an additional art teacher and was an instant hit with young girls, hormones raging and starved of any male presence. A novelty and most popular in our year.

Sharpe, Aunty Audrey and Uncle Lionel. Mum's cousin was Lionel and with Audrey, his wife, they owned an electrical goods/ironmongers/haberdashery shop in Crowland until they suddenly left and went to live in Eastbourne.

Sismore, Terry and Doreen and son Michael, friends of my parents who lived at 35 Sherborne Road, Peterborough.

Taylor, Anne. Schoolfriend from 3A1 who used to live on Eastern Avenue so I cycled with her at lunch time to reach my Grandparents' house at 11 Briar Way.

Tendera, Vicky, school friend in my class, 3A2 who lived at 37 Ash Close, Dogsthorpe, Peterborough. I was her bridesmaid in 1971.

Vickers, Jean was on the same 2 year Commercial Course at me at Tech. college. I became very good friends with her, and sister Jane, 4 years later when we met up again on the dance floor at the A1 club at RAF Wittering.

Violet, Great Aunty and Grandma's sister lived at Whaplode Drove or Shepeau Stow.

Walker, Jean, my Dad's Aunty and mother to Hannah Allen and Robert Walker. She lived with her husband and son Robert at 39 Balmerino Road, Douglas & Angus, Dundee, Scotland. We often went round at the weekend for tea and met up with the Healeys and a lady called Ann. (photo)

Wright, Janet and Charles (painter and decorater) and baby Oliver. Friends of parents who lived at 9 Grassmere Gardens, Gunthorpe.

Quotes from some of the 'old girls' on the Facebook page "John Mansfield school 1960-1970":-

Caroline: "I was good at gym but hated hockey and that hockey ball hurt if it hit you. I used to end up running away from it and mrs Handley shouting at me to run towards the ball not away."

Lynda: "Miss Franks wrote on my report, 'This child is erratic'. Which was all very well and didn't seem to adversely bother my parents. But, I, whilst not knowing the word erratic, did know the word erotic and in my mind confused the two (I had just read a rude book as 13 year olds do) I worried about this for quite a while. . . ."

Lynda: "I too had Miss Roberts for History. When she caught me passing notes along the back row in the classroom, she hauled me out of my chair and dragged me to the front of the class (minus my shoes which were still under my desk). After that I had to sit at the front for all of her lessons. My history knowledge improved after that . ."

Lynda: "Oh yes, I'm an authority on ' Hill Forts' and 'strip farming' . . . . Chuckle."

Sally: "Lynda you could write a best selling humorous book on your time at John Mansfield. Lol erratic/erotic naughty books and being pulled to the front of the class minus shoes."

Lynda: "I'm sure I could, when I left, I left ' charlie' the skeleton in the science room in his cupboard dressed in my school uniform, complete with hockey boots around his neck. And, before you ask, yes he was wearing his beret."

Cathy: "Miss Roberts was our form teacher in the fourth year someone dared me to lock her in the cupboard (the one between history room and French room) of course I did then I daren't let her out! Miss Newborn certainly made my wrists hurt that day happy memories."

Sally: "Did you get lines? I don't remember any corporal punishment, as that was more in primary school!"

Cathy: "No Sally I got the ruler over the back of my wrists."

Lesley: "I remember Miss Franks and her little sports car. Once a girl was caught chewing gum, she made her sit with it on her nose throughout the lesson. We couldn't work for sniggering."

Sally: "Does anyone remember a specific book at school? I only remember this one in the school library, when Mrs. Barber taught us. I probably only remember it because it has a cover picture of Patti Boyd, the wife of Beatle George Harrison. Also I've just located old copies on Abe Books from £2.80 so I've bought one to find out what I should have been doing at 15."

Lynn: "Only paperback I remember from around my school days (apart from English Lit list!) was Suedehead and others of a similar type, sold at Boots but think they were banned at JM."

Sally: "Jelly Bean Bags were fashionable for taking books around in school until we made tie dye, drawstring bags in art which served the purpose. Carrying satchells around school was discouraged as the buckles could scratch the walls."

Lynda: "My worse memory is (because I was talking) I was shut in the music cupboard by Miss Bex, the music teacher. She forgot I was there and I sat in the cupboard, too afraid to come out, for the whole of the next lesson and didn't come out until lunch time when it all went quiet."

Caroline: "Oh Lynda that was awful. Miss Bex was known to hate children. How she became a teacher I'll never know. I can remember if you forgot your recorder you had to go into the cupboard and use a ruler as if it was a recorder. I really wonder why they treated us like that. It's no wonder parents now stand no nonsense from teachers. It's probably because they were treated badly as a child. Good for your mum Brenda that teacher deserved it. I don't think I even told my mum."

Brenda: "Lol I was so scared when mum went down the school, I thought she would be arrested. I think that's why I'm claustrophobic and cant be in small spaces, I start panicking!"

Lynda: "The Miss Bex story got worse. On a parents' evening, my Mum and Dad were talking to this really nice teacher. . . Mum says the one Lynda really can't stand is Miss Bex. . . . Yup you guessed it! It didn't improve my music lessons!"

Sally: "Does anyone know or remember what happened to Helen Tubb? She was a pupil at John Mansfield school and was made to eat her lunch on school wall as packed lunches were not allowed in school ? Parents had a note pinned to her coat saying "Helen Tubbs mobile canteen" (1970 - 1975). It was even featured on ITV. I'd love to know how the school responded as I had to go to a friend's house or cycle to my Grandma's to eat my packed lunch."

Sue: "Was our school song 'Go Forth With God'?

Romayne: I didn't even realise we had one!

Sally: I remember being woken up for school in Winter when you could see your breath and there was ice on the inside of the windows. Mum used to have a paraffin heater on in the kitchen with our clothes next to it ready. My friend used to get dressed in bed and my husband said they had a one bar wall heater in each bedroom which was too expensive to use except for 5 minutes to get dressed! What are your memories pre central heating?"

Brenda: "We had a coal fire downstairs. The "front room" fire was only lit at Christmas. We only had an outside toilet and dad brought the zinc bath tub into the kitchen on a Sunday night and it was filled with hot water from a gas copper. I was the youngest so first in the bath (but I was probably the dirtiest)! A very happy childhood though and nothing but praise for my fantastic mum and dad."

Lynda: "Much the same as the above, ice on the inside of the windows. Bowl to catch the water one year when the roof tiles had slipped and water coming thru the ceiling. Coats on the beds as all the blankets were very thin. Cardboard in my shoes when they got a hole in the sole. Why do I moan about anything at all now, because I don't think we moaned about it at the time, just got on with it!"

Elizabeth: "Ice on the inside of the windows and the curtains frozen to the glass."

Brenda: "We didn't have duvets in them days,it was flannette sheets .blankets and an eiderdown to keep us warm. My mum had a flatly drier and put clothes on the sticks then put a lid on it lol. Paraffin heater for when we had a bath."

Sandra: "I had my grannie's fur coat on top of the eiderdown. I remember feathers used to poke through the mattress and pillows."

Shirley: "We had out side toilet and took bucket with old on for up stairs, those were the days ha ha."

Shirley: "Meant bucket with lid on ha ha that's why I was in a C class."

Caroline: "We had metal framed windows so ice used to form on the inside. The patterns that formed were really beautiful. I remember I used to stand and look at them. We too had a paraffin heater which, when we were young used to get dressed in front of, but as we got older we got dressed in the cold. It never took long to put our clothes on. We used to have a man deliver the paraffin. We had it in a large bottle and it was pink. We had an inside bathroom but having a bath in the winter was a nightmare. The bathroom never seemed to get warm."

Sheila: "We had a coal fire and in the bathroom we had a light with a two ring heater, one pull light, two pull heater & light, three pull heater four pull off."

Sally: "I started a two year 'commercial course' at Tech. College in 1968, shorthand typing, office practice, book keeping, commerce, English and geography. Miss Longhorn was our typing teacher."

Brenda: "Wednesday was half day closing in Peterborough. I got a holiday job as a shampoo girl in Mrs Gore's hairdressers on Lincoln Road Millfield which was great then when I started on a two year full-time course at Peterborough Tech doing secretarial and office practice, Mrs Gore had to "let me go" as I wasn't doing hairdressing which was a bummer really as that is when I really needed the money. Mrs Gore was nice though and even bought me a wedding present."

Jennifer: "I got a Saturday job at Woolworths, remember it well, the old wooden floors Xmas cards sold singley biscuits also sold as pick and mix."

Linda: "I got a Saturday/holiday job in the local paper shop, very handy just round the corner!"

Brenda: "My Saturday job was Colton cycles Toy dept in Hereward Cross, loved it ."

Sue: "Sheltons restaurant and Purdys were my Sat jobs no wonder I ended up catering as a career."

Eileen: "Wednesday still is half day closing in Holbeach, my local town .. I was 15 in 1966 and I remember going to the arcade agency at some point...in Sept 66 I started full time at Perkins as many of us did who didn't stay on to do exams.."

Sally: "Interesting that 'half day closing' survives in rural places."

Sandra: "There were a few of us from John Mansfield that worked at the Bulb Factory at Werrington on a Saturday and school holidays. I became allergic to Hyacinth bulbs."

Elizabeth: "Saturday job at Fairways."

Sue: "Combex? Werrington on the toy spraying conveyor belts... such a laugh more paint on us than the toys!!!"

Brenda: "Fairways was my fulltime job Elizabeth for 5yrs when I left school in 1968!"

Norma: "Saturday job at Rebecca Jane hairdressers (first floor above where Genevas Bar is now in Geneva Street) at 14. Heather who owned the shop was a family friend and knew I was looking for a job. I stayed there right through my year at College and only gave it up when I started my first full time job as a secretary at Rigby Williams & Co solicitors (corner of Craig Street and Lincoln Road, now turned into yet more flats) as I had to work Saturday mornings."

Sally: "Which course did you do at College Norma? Did it start in 1968?"

Norma: "One year audio typists course Sally. I was signed up to a 2 year hairdressing course but, as my arthritis was getting worse, a career change was needed sharpish! The audio typists, was the only one left. Thought I'd hate it but loved it. 1969."

Sally: "Worked out well then, and we were at College at the same time. I left in the Summer of 1970 and started work at the Town Clerk's Dept., Town Hall. You had to work a 5 and a half day week?" Norma: "Five and a half day week every other week. An amazing workload but it improved my typing speed which was useful when I moved to the BBC and helped out in the News Room! My first day at Rigbys was taking statements from clients on remand in Bedford Prison - talk about jumping in at the deep end!"

Sally: "Wow, I was just about to mention the deep end! And on manual typewriters, with several carbon copies, to rub out mistakes which were inevitable! Character building stuff!"

Norma: "Certainly was!"

Jennifer: "Sally you must have known my dad he was mayor in 1970 Roy Topley."

Sally: "Yes, the name does ring a bell but our legal office was out of the way of the Mayor's Parlour where Jean and Jenny worked, the Mayor's secretarial staff."

Sally: "This reminds me of school. 'Yet another day has gone by where I've not had to use algebra, make a Venn diagram or had to set fire to magnesium on a Bunsen burner.' This came up on my Facebook feed. Laptops, Ipads, Ipods, something we could never have contemplated back in the day!"

Sally: "I'm in the process of transcribing my 1967 diary and my recollection of Miss Newborn is that she wore a stiff dull green dress with a shirt type top and matching belt where she used to fold over a little embroidered handkerchief. Some times a tweed suit. Always very smart and slim. The police came on one occasion when something was written about her in yellow paint on the walls which we were not allowed to see!"

Jennifer: "I remember her at lunch time if she sat at your table she told you after every mouth full of food you should count to ten between each mouthful to aid the digestive system."

Caroline: "Does anyone remember the day that someone tied a bra to the netball post in the playground and the whole school had to sit in the hall as Miss Newborn called the police to find out who did it. I never did hear who tied it there. Good Times."

Chris: "I remember that I do know who did it.... No not me .. Not mentioning her name on FB though will tell you when we meet again. I saw Miss Schneider (can't spell her name) last week. Had a little chat to her about JM."

Unfortunately for some reason I was away from school when the photo was taken in our first year 1964/65.

MISS MALSTERS CLASS 1A (2) FIRST YEAR AT JOHN MANSFIELD SCHOOL.

L-R FRONT ROW
ELIZABETH DAVIDSON, ANNE WALKER, VALERIE TATAM, PAULINE MURDIN, JANET EDWARDS, KATHLEEN WESTOBY, LESLEY SANDFORD.

2ND ROW
BARBARA BRUCE, BETTY BOINTON, LYN BOOCOCK, SUSAN SNAPE, SUSAN PRITCHARD, LYNDA PARKER, ANGELA DEWDNEY, STEPHANIE JACKSON, BARBARA MONDAY.

3RD ROW
CAROL EDIS, STEPHANIE BABBS, DENISE GRAY, GAIL PAINTIN.

BACK ROW
SUSAN BOOLS, HILARY HARRISON, BRONWEN BIRCH, CAROL CUNNINGHAM, ANNE HARRISON, SUSAN DAVIS, SUSAN HARRIS, VICKY TENDERA, CATHY BILSBY.

It must have been the late 1960s when Dr. Scholl's wooden exercise sandals came into fashion and I am seen wearing these in the photo on the front cover. Another friend I met on Facebook from the same era and from Peterborough also wore Scholl sandals and her comment brought back memories. Caroline:- "I did lose one once on the way to holiday camp. It dropped between the platform and the train (mind the gap!), but my friend's Dad rescued it for me. I hated when they'd slip and all of a sudden you'd get that wooden heel back on your instep."

Thursday 12th
Brenda bought me this Diary. Didn't get humps until afternoon break. Had needlework Exam. Got more bumps in the Gym when all the class joined in. I saw the film of the Monkees to the tune of "I'm a Believer", it was fab, great, lovely! I saw it on 'Top of the Pops'.

Friday 13th
Miss Harkin came back. Ann fell in a puddle and got all wet. Mrs. Barber did not have my scarf. I saw part of the Monkees act on 'Junior Points of View'. Heard Monkees theme music on wireless. Mmmmmmm.

Saturday 14th
I got a new dress from Roses,[the dress shop on the corner of the Westgate Arcade]. *Got another scarf. Saw Carol Gifford in town. Mum had a tooth out early morning. Saw 3rd Monkees programme and taped it. Came out good. Davy was fab so was Peter, Mike and Micky.*

Sunday 15th
Washed hair. Played Monkees taped programme nearly all day. I did a bit of revising, helped Ian with a jigsaw puzzle. Went to cousin Jill's for tea at night. The children were noisy and I had a bad headache there.

Monday 16th
I got prepared for exams at school, Ann Foster rode to school with me on her bike. Penfriend Barby Matson [44 Circuit Road, Chestnut Hill, Massachusetts] *wrote to me and she likes the Monkees. Read a rotten article about them in the Sunday Mirror that was unfair. I went to see 'Sound of Music' at the Odeon, it was lovely.*

Tuesday 17th
The exams started today but they were not too bad. Lost my ruler. Nothing special happened much.

Wednesday 18th
School was not too bad on 2nd day of exams. I got the Lady Penelope magazine with Monkees in colour. They have been No. 1 since Sunday. Nothing much happened again.

Thursday 19th
Science exam was terrible, it lasted 2 hours. Got called out in assembly by Miss Newborn, I was scared stiff, but the groundsman had found my ruler and

given it to her. Brenda said I could go to her party. Saw film of Monkees on Top of the Pops. It was similar to the beginning of their programme.

Friday 20th

History Exam terrible. Finished Housecraft exam half an hour before time. I went to see the Pantomime 'Robinson Crusoe' at the Embassy with Anne and little sister Sue. Jess Conrad was lovely, screamed at him. Dad brought home recording of 'Sound of Music'.

Saturday 21st

Did not go to town but Mum did. Washed and set hair, came out O.K. Dad and Mum took Topsy to the vet and she was all right. Taped Monkees programme but it wasn't as good as usual, I don't know why.

Sunday 22nd

I had a lovely Sunday. Went to Church. Not much homework only to revise Geography. Wrote out two thank-you letters. [The only other young person at the church evening service was David but I was never introduced nor ever dared speak to him as I thought it would ruin my chances!]

Monday 23rd

Ended the exams today with a 2 hour Geography exam (oh boy!).

Tuesday 24th

Anne was not at school, had cold. Brenda gave me a Milky bar, 2nd day running. Dad brought me a cutting about the Monkees from 'The Sketch' from work. Liz and Dave [Langfield, friends of parents 77 Priory Road, Peterborough] *came at night.*

Wednesday 25th

Sorted out readings with Mrs. Burt in double maths lesson. Rained in morning got soaked. Brenda & I got bumps. Got invitation to Brenda's party. Miss Harkin said she wanted to see our French projects. I hadn't even started mine so had loads to do at night on it.

Thursday 26th

Got our first results (English). Had plays with Miss Harkin for exams - couldn't remember my lines. Got indigestion. Saw 'Top of Pops' with Monkees from a bit of last programme.

Friday 27th

I got a letter from Simon [2nd cousin]. *Rained. Cleaned out lockers at school. Nothing much happened.*

Saturday 28th

Washed hair but came out terrible. Went to town and got some 'Countess' hair conditioner. Ian got a chemistry set. The Monkees was ever so good but could not tape it 'cos Brenda's Dad and Moira came. I had good fun playing with Ian's chemistry set.

Sunday 29th

Wasn't so good weekend as last. Went to church by myself, was O.K. Ian made some INVISIBLE ink with his chemistry set.

Monday 30th January, 1967

"Anne came back today. Heard about the police raid at the Crown. Nothing much really happened."

Tuesday 31st

Had hockey (ugh!). I was goal-keeper but never even touched the ball. I heard about some Monkees songs. 'Last Train To Clarksville' going back into the hit parade now that 'I'm a Believer' is No. 1. Vicky told me about the flip side being 'I'm not your stepping stone'. Brenda recited a few words and music to 'This just isn't my day'.

February

Wednesday 1st

School dentist came but I did not see him. Miss Beckwith came but did not see her. I got a late mark in the afternoon just coming back from dinner. Rang Brenda who had xray on foot but just badly bruised.

Thursday 2nd

School dentist came, had to see him, said mouth overcrowded and I've got to have some teeth out. Miss Harkin ordered me to do speech on Paris Project. Queer things went on with Ann and Butcher Boy. Top of the Pops only showed pictures of the Monkees and no film.

Friday 3rd

Said my speech in French, it was not too bad. Stuck Monkees on locker door yesterday. Rather a windy day.

Saturday 4th

Ian was very poorly and sick in the night and all of today. Dad and I went to town. Could not get 'Musical Express' 'cos they had sold out 'cos of Monkees. Taped the programme successfully though.

Sunday 5th

Cleaned bike a bit and Ian seemed better. Grandma and Grandpa came. Couldn't go to church 'cos when I got there I couldn't get the door open! Ian was ill again at night time.

Monday 6th

Had headache and sore throat. Ian never went to school but much better at night. My book from the library is called 'Jamaica Inn' [by Daphne Du Maurier]. Shocking surprize about Ann and information from Lesley.

Tuesday 7th

Ended up with rotten bad cold. Heard about Micky Dolenz who had just arrived in England. Pancake day and had one at night.

Wednesday 8th

Got headache in afternoon. Went to bed early. Heard about Mike and wife Phyllis just came over here and pic of Micky and Paul in Daily Mirror. Chatted to Aunt Dora when waiting for my "Lady Penny".

Thursday 9th

Started reading "Jamaica Inn" yesterday. Science was good with bottles and test tubes. Cold still bad. "Top of Pops" lovely with Micky & Mike.

Friday 10th

Angela got me a NME [New Musical Express] and a Radio Times with Monkees in. Gave Brenda bumps. Most of class went to night dance at Lincoln Road Boys School with Sounds. I did a competition in "Lady Penny".

Saturday 11th BRENDA'S BIRTHDAY.

Had hair done at "Jane's" in morning. Looked nice. Went to Brenda's party in afternoon it was fab. Danced a lot. Went to Gran's afterwards [11 Briar Way, Peterborough]. Brenda swapped her silver stockings with me but I laddered them.

Sunday 12th

Ann F. bought back my "Pinky Blues" [lipstick]. Liz and Dave came when Mum and I were getting ready for church. We went to church though it was good. Read more of "Jamaica Inn". Didn't think much to Mum's home made syrup pud.

Monday 13th

Day off from school 'cos of half term. Posted Dad's valentine cards. Ann F. wanted me to go to town with her. Jill came with David. Played a short game of Monopoly. Davy Jones came over today from U.S.

Tuesday 14th

Valentine's day. Dad got a card and Mum got Dad's. At school everyone said my hair looked nice. Not much in paper about Davy Jones. Dad puzzled about his valentine card. Monkees not No. 1 any more. It is instead Petula Clark, 'This is my 'Song'.

Wednesday 15th

Had student for French. Brenda not at school. Spent Netball lessons blowing up balls. Had a lot of homework at night. Hair still looked nice. Window cleaners came.

Thursday 16th

Picture of Davy Jones in Daily Mirror on a horse. Played recorders in prayers. Hair went curlier and frizzier. Brenda still not at school and Debbie was off. Got free hair conditioner from "Jackie" magazine.

Friday 17th

Miss Harkin gave us a lecture about cleanliness and tidiness. Rained all day. Went to see "My Fair Lady" at the Embassy at night.

Saturday 18th

Forgot to write my Diary. Never went to town. Washed hair. Dad went bowling at night at Corby. Taped Monkees. Got part of "This just doesn't seem to be my day" from wireless.

Sunday 19th

Rained a lot. Had loads of homework. Mr. and Mrs. Hasty came. [Chick and Gracie friends of parents who lived at 52 Priory Road, Peterborough and children were Linda, and twins Colin and Gillian]. *Went to church by myself.*

Monday 20th Schools Birthday.
Rained quite a bit didn't get wet much. Had Royal Band in morning 'cos school's birthday. Vicky was lovesick. Anne Taylor went to dentist in afternoon.

Tuesday 21st
We had some March winds and April showers. Saw true story of Madeline Smith on telly. Nothing much happened.

Wednesday 22nd
Got Monkees fan club address off Kathy W. Wrote to it at night. Nothing much happened.

Thursday 23rd
Prizegiving. Had a few lessons off in afternoon. We had a lady who came to watch Miss Shilt teach us.

Friday 24th
Hilary Harrison's birthday. Washed hair and had bath. Davy Jones on "Junior Points of View". Mum went in full-time at work.

Saturday 25th
Got fed up with nothing to do. Taped Monkees programme, it was ever so good and sad. Finished "Jamaica Inn". Just found out that it was George Harrison's birthday. [Beatles]

Sunday 26th
Did homework most of the day. Gran came and Mum gave her some coats. Went to church by myself. Telly broke down but it was only the wire.

Monday 27th
Rained and became very windy towards dinner time. Got book out of library called "Rebecca". [Daphne Du Maurier]

Tuesday 28th
Dad took us in the car to school. Nurse came. Traffic stopped on High Street at lunchtime because church steeple was swaying.

March

Wednesday 1st
Got our reports. Had test on "Jane Eyre". Steeplejacks went to church. Played skipping. Cathy got 'Athlete's hand and mouth' illness.

Thursday 2nd

Didn't have needlework 'cos Miss Wakelin was not there. Thought I saw Uncle Roy [Eggleshaw from Nottingham, friend of parents] *passing the High Street. Mum found out about the Youth Club for me and got me fixed up to go.*

Friday 3rd

Things went wrong for me in the morning. Got Saturday's plans settled but only 3 out of 5 coming. Got loads of homework. Puncture.

Saturday 4th

Got puffed out cleaning up this morning. Mum had hair done at Jane's 'cos went to dance at Tec. [College] I had some friends in, Ann H., Vicky and Brenda played records and we danced. It was o.k.

Sunday 5th MOTHER'S DAY

Took Brenda back about 11 a.m. Got on with my loads of homework. Had 3 lots of visitors, Mr. & Mrs. Bedford & Vicki, Grandma & Grandpa & Brenda's Dad with Moira and Annette. Went to church and felt sick.

Monday 6th

Felt a bit ill in morning. Got out early at dinner time because of commonwealth visitors. It was quite good in the afternoon. Miss Harkin had had her hair cut differently.

Tuesday 7th

Anne Taylor had her valve pinched off her bike the night before. Got finger bashed in hockey and it swelled a little. Went to Youth Club at night [in Leeds Hall, High Street, Eye]. It was terrible and I'm never going' again. [Got hit by flying table tennis balls and the darts were going everywhere.]

Wednesday 8th

Ann Walker's mother came to the school about Ann's report. Miss Harkin apologized. Dad had to walk home because his bike was pinched. He said whoever had it would not know that the brakes had never worked!

Thursday 9th

First time "Jackie" had anything in about Monkees. Had to play netball instead of Gym because workmen were repairing apparatus. Nothing special happened. Anne Taylor got her bike going.

Friday 10th

Tidied out Miss Harkin's drawer in form period. Heard about girl getting expelled from school. Nothing much happened at all.

Saturday 11th
Went to town. Got a "Model Girl" No 1. Monkees were good this week. I love Micky's impression of James Cagney.

Sunday 12th
Hadn't much homework to do 'cos did most of it Friday night. Had to get house spick & span. In afternoon we had the Green's and Grandma and Grandpa to tea. Had stomach ache at night and got to bed late.

Monday 13th
Lesley S. & I giggled a lot. A lot of stock taking was being done. Ian had a hair cut. That is all except I wrote to caravan sites about holidays.

Tuesday 14th
Had Mrs. Whiting instead of Mrs. Halse in Housecraft Theory. She said we had a good chance of having cookery next term. Nothing much happened.

Wednesday 15th
Mrs Burt was away so it was a lovely Maths lesson. My pen wouldn't write. Had argument with Kathy W. in netball. Woke up last night and night before. Last night when I woke I had to make my bed 'cos all the covers were on the floor. Dad phoned up about some holiday bungalows but could not get one. They were near Yarmouth.

Thursday 16th
Heard about Mrs Brown & Miss Whiteford who are leaving and Miss Cowling for six months. Had a shipwreck in Gym. Last lesson with Miss Child for French. School bag split had to carry books in my arms.

Friday 17th St. Patrick's Day
Morning was good. Auntie Sheila was at Grandma's with Sharon. Holiday things came but Dad booked up on the phone to California Cliffs. Washed hair & used setting lotion from "Model Girl".

Saturday 18th
Got wallpaper off one wall in room. Did not go to town. Mum bought me a "Meet the Monkees" from the Post Office and they were good on T.V. Dad went bowling at night.

Sunday 19th
I did homework it wasn't much. Mowed lawn with Ian. Grandma and Grandpa came. Had fritters for tea. Did not go to church. Put the clocks on last night.

Monday 20th
Gave my tape to Vicky to tape the Monkees L.P. When I got home there was tape from cousin Jill, it was very nice. Mum got her grey suit.

Tuesday 21st
Brought my tortoise home. Lesley brought some lovely frost lipstick to school. Vicky brought my tape back with Monkees LP on it. Last lesson of hockey. It seemed a very hot day.

Wednesday 22nd
Moved to Rm. 10. Broke up from school. got our new timetable. Most of school leavers cried. Ian and I got Easter eggs from Auntie Jean in Dundee. Cracked my tooth a bit on the ball.

Thursday 23rd (Maundy Thursday)
Spent a long time weeding the gravel for Dad. Ate Ian's Easter egg 'cos it was broken. Wrote two letters to "Model Girl". Ian cut the grass I played on my skates.

Friday 24th (Good Friday)
Got worn out pulling remains of wall paper off room walls. Grandma & Grandpa came and gave us a 1/- [1 shilling i.e. 10p] bar of chocolate each for Easter. Washed hair (came out nice) and had a bath.

Saturday 25th
Went to town. Brierley's was horrible and crowded. Weighed myself and was upset because I was nearly 9 st. Went to Gran's. Bought 'Petticoat'. Dad bought silver-grey paint from Brierleys to do the woodwork in. Bought Anne's birthday present. It was a 'One & Only' all in one makeup and nylons.

Sunday 26th
Helped a little with the back garden which we did most of the day. Went to church with Mum even though Gran & Grandpa came. Ate Easter egg. Church was decorated in lovely Spring flowers.

Monday 27th
Did garden only a bit. Had bit of a sprained wrist. Liz & Dave came at night and took Mum & Dad to the "Fitzwilliam Arms". Saw a film while they were gone called "The Nun's Story" with Audrey Hepburn. It was very good. Bed. 12.55 a.m.

Tuesday 28th
Had letter from Uncle Angus to say that he was coming down. Hailed a lot. took Mum to work & went to town. Spent 5s that Auntie Margaret sent for

Easter on some lip stuff. Got a book from the Library called "Gone With The Wind". Got a telegram from Uncle Angus. Dad phoned up Granddad. All was fixed & OK. Bed. 11.40 p.m.

Wednesday 29th
Got up late. Read to end of part 1 in "Gone With The Wind". Wanted to play tennis but could not find ball. Helped Mum with the "Weekend" competition. Did not do much. Bed: 11.55 p.m.

Thursday 30th
Had bath, washed hair. Uncle Angus and Cousin Shonagh arrived at 4 p.m. Felt sick through eating too many sweets. My legs ached. Bed:9.30 p.m.

Friday 31st
Got up at 8 o'clock. Went to Park with Uncle Angus and Shonagh, then to bowling alley. Had dinner at Co-op. Went home. Later went to bowling alley again with Dad. Met Mum in town. Did some shopping. Bed: 11:15 p.m.

April

Saturday 1st
Mum's trees arrived and were planted by Dad & Uncle Angus. We did some shopping and got wallpaper for living room. Went to bowling alley. Had chicken for tea only I never had any. I watched the Monkees while the grown-ups went to "Fitzwilliam Arms".

Sunday 2nd *Anne's birthday*
Had bad headache. Went to Gran's for 1 min. Went to Auntie Sheila's and all grown-ups went to pub while I looked after all the children. Picked Mum up and went to bowling alley. Couldn't go to church 'cos stayed at Bowl.

Monday 3rd
Had bad headache all day. Uncle Angus went back to Scotland and left loads of things behind. Did not do much except help cut the grass. Went to bed early forgot to write my diary.

Tuesday 4th
Got up late. Cleaned out top drawer of dressing table. Found the McDonald Crest ring. Grandpa came. Heard the Monkees new record "A little bit me, a little bit you" at Auntie Sheila's on Sunday for first time. Bed: 11:35 p.m.

Wednesday 5th
Shone up McDonald crest ring up and wore it. Did mostly my Paris thing all day. My right arm ached a lot. Brenda's Dad and Maura came at night.

Thursday 6th

Couldn't get boiler fire to go all afternoon. Tacked hem on my mauve dress. Did a bit more of Paris. Mum's fir trees came in the afternoon. Watched "Top of Pops".

Friday 7th

Went to town in the morning got things for school and Ian's new shoes. In the afternoon cleared house up. Read quite of a bit of "Gone With the Wind" after having it re-dated at library. Bed: 11.45 p.m.

Saturday 8th

Candidates for voting came round. Cleared most of furniture out of room. Read a little too much of "Gone with the Wind". Eurovision song contest on and Sandie Shaw won singing 'Puppet on a String'. Grand National was on too. Bed: 12.30 a.m.

Sunday 9th

Washed down and started painting room. Made a chocolate sponge for Mum. Grandma & Grandpa came. Went to church by myself. Taped the Monkees new song from Radio London. Saw funny film at night on A.T.V. Bed: 12 p.m.

Monday 10th

Last day of freedom. Rained all day. Did not do much. Bed: 10:5 p.m.

Tuesday 11th

Went back to school. Gave Anne Taylor her birthday present. Ann Foster didn't turn up at school because she thought she didn't have to go back until tomorrow. It was Budget day. Bed: 10:9 p.m.

Wednesday 12th

Was not a bad day. Came home from school on the main road with Ann. Mum got a new suit. Bed: 10:12 p.m.

Thursday 13th

It was polling day at Eye. Dad had his car tested. Nothing much happened. Bed: 10:16 p.m.

Friday 14th

Was not all that nice today at school. My hair looked terrible, washed it at night. Got a new form captain. Dad went out at night. Got car taxed. Bed: 10:55 p.m.

Saturday 15th

Went to town for about half an hour in afternoon. Got a "Model Girl". Dad went bowling at night. Bed: 11:50 p.m.

Sunday 16th

Had a tiring day. Simon & Andrew, Auntie Doris and Auntie Lil came unexpected in morning. Went to hills & hollows at Barnack in afternoon. [Otherwise known as 'Hills and Holes Nature Reserve' and from Wikipedia there is an explanation:- 'The unique hummocky landscape was created by quarrying for limestone. The stone, sometimes known as Barnack Rag, was a valuable building stone first exploited by the Romans over 1,500 years ago. Most famously, stone from Barnack was used to build Peterborough and Ely Cathedrals. By the year 1500 however, all the useful stone had been removed and the bare heaps of limestone rubble gradually became covered by the rich carpet of wild flowers that can be seen today.'] *At night Mum's friends came Mr and Mrs Partridge & Julia.*
Bed:10:0p.m.

Monday 17th

Had a horrible night. Today the sun was shining, it was hot, Miss Harkin was not at school & it was a glorious day. Had first cookery lesson since 2nd year. Mum had a day off to do papering but Dad just finished off paintwork. Bed: 9:55 p.m.

Tuesday 18th

It was a much colder day & Miss Harkin came back. Mum did some wallpapering. First game of tennis & etc. since last summer. Bed: 10:25 p.m.

Wednesday 19th

It was choir festival for our school and Eye. Mum went back to work & did a bit of wallpapering first. Nothing much happened. Bed: 10:18 p.m.

Thursday 20th

Science was good we took our temperatures and mine was 97.3. We also cut up a bull's eye. Bronwen brought her transistor in Needlework. Threw the javelin in Athletics. Rained at night. Bed: 10:40 p.m.

Friday 21st

Paid my money to go to see film. Queen's Birthday. Yesterday girls in 4th year took Tec. entrance exam at the college. It was Vicky's housewarming party. Washed hair and did history homework. Bed: 11:25 p.m.

Saturday 22nd

Went to dentist. Had bad headache all day. Auntie Sheila, Mrs Lane, Graham & Sharon came for a few minutes. Mum did some more wallpapering. Dad did a bit more to the tiles in bathroom. Bed: 11:40 p.m.

Sunday 23rd

It was St. George's Day. Mum & Dad got room straightened. Did not have much homework to do as I did history Friday night. Mrs. Hasty & Linda came about 7.30 p.m. as Linda was going Nursing. Never went to church. Bed: 10:55 p.m.

Monday 24th

Mum had her hair done at "Jane's" and brought me back some hair spray. Nothing much happened. Bed: 10:20 p.m.

Tuesday 25th

Dad took us to school in the morning 'cos it rained. Games were horrible because we had a race. Saw a good film on telly at night called "Female on the Beach." Bed: 10.35 p.m.

Wednesday 26th

It was rather a warm day. Mrs. [Mabel] Noble was at Grandma's. Ann liked Mum's red amaryllis lily. Nothing much happened. Bed: 10:12 p.m.

Thursday 27th

Took my transistor to school so it was quite good. The street lights at Newark Avenue were turned on for the first time. Played tennis in athletics. Bed: 10:20 p.m.

Friday 28th

Had two films and a tape recording in morning. Mrs. Burt got very mad and red faced in Maths (Geometry). Rained a bit but was warm. Washed hair. Watched Miss England on telly. Miss Nottingham won. Bed: 11:45 p.m.

Saturday 29th

Went to town & to Grandma's. Got a bag for Phyllis. Did a bit of gardening after. Mum & Dad went out for about an hour at night.

Sunday 30th

Spent most of the day helping with garden and patio. Mr. Abbott came in morning to ask if we wanted to go out. We were going to Auntie Lucy's but didn't. Took dog with Ian & looked round Laurel Farm Estate. Bed 10.45 p.m.

May

Monday 1st
It snowed and thundered a bit on & off. Had letter from Monkees fan club & a slimming leaflet. Mum had a "Philippot" arrive. Bed: 9:55 p.m.

Tuesday 2nd
Exam with Miss Franks so had to have Mr. Scot. Head wind cycling both ways. Mum & Dad had cornish pasties, too much pastry. Saw rather good film called "It happened one night" with Claudette Colbert & Clark Gable. Bed: 10:35 p.m.

Wednesday 3rd
Had to go to library at afternoon break to discuss plans for "Richard III". Was exams in music room. Nothing much happened.

Thursday 4th
"Richard III was boring. got back to school at 12:15 p.m. Late for dinner, had to rush down Eastern Ave (head wind). Rained. Miss Wakelin away for needlework had Miss Harper didn't do much. Joined in with Class 1C with a kind of rounders in Gym. Bed: 10:17 p.m.

Friday 5th
Rained a lot. A pop quiz in music. Washed hair. Dad went & looked at another car. Nothing much happened. Bed:

Saturday 6th
Hair came out quite nice. Went to town but didn't stop long. Mum had hair done at "Thelma's" wasn't very good. Monkees were good. Mum & Dad went out at night and enjoyed themselves. Bed: 12:40 a.m.

Sunday 7th
There were lots of April showers. Did some homework. Gran & Grandpa came. Mum & I went to church. Dad had a headache at night. Bed: 10:55 p.m.

Monday 8th
Had sore throat in the morning. Nothing much happened. Bed: 10:20 p.m.

Tuesday 9th
Susan Bools birthday she got a guitar and I helped pay for a record. Didn't have a very nice games lesson. Was a hot day. Polling but mum didn't go. A mixed up film on the telly. Bed: 10:16 p.m.

Wednesday 10th
It was a very hot day. Didn't have my coat on at dinner time. Ann bought me an ice-lolly on way home. Had a test in history. Bed: 11:10 p.m.

Thursday 11th
Had day off 'cos of polling. In the morning I was all on my todd. Went to Kathy's party in afternoon. Had headache & cramp at night. Gran & Grandpa came. Cat fish died and was buried. Bed: 10:20 p.m.

Friday 12th
Had horrible headache in morning. Queer things went on in Room 14. Had Geography in Gym. Miss Harkin was late in afternoon. Talked to Brenda. Washed hair. Rained and thundered just after break in afternoon. Got soaked on way home. Bed: 11:25 p.m.

Saturday 13th
Went to town in afternoon. Monkees were good. Dad went bowling at night. Thundered about half past seven time. Nothing special happened. Bed: 11:40 p.m.

Sunday 14th
Rained all day. Did not do much. Did not do any homework 'cos did it Friday night. Made some cheese scones. Went to Mrs. Bedford's & Mrs. Cranswick's. Saw last episode of "St. Ives". Bed: 11 p.m.

Monday 15th
Dad went to London. Poured with rain all afternoon. Bacon & egg pie was quite good. Got a lot of folders. Nothing much really happened. Bed: 10: 40 p.m.

Tuesday 16th
In double games had to have two games of rounders because grass too wet to play Athletics. Lesley P. walked home with us. Discussed emigrating to Canada & Dad's trip to London. Got ever so excited at night. Dad set grass seed. Bed: 10:45 p.m.

Wednesday 17th
Ann F's birthday. Drizzled in morning so went by car. Picked up Ann's cards from postman on way. Talked a little about Canada. Got more leaflets on it. Bed: 10:15 p.m.

Thursday 18th
Came home at dinner time 'cos had stomach ache went back though. Gran & Grandpa came at night. Got letter of hair-style to suit my shape of face, back from magazine Bed 10:30 p.m.

Friday 19th

Bought first copy of "All our own". Washed hair at night. Rained hard at dinner time. Cleaned bedroom thoroughly and did some of my homework. Bed 12:20 a.m.

Saturday 20th

Hair came out nice. Was very windy. Had a quick visit uptown. Cup final on telly against Spurs & Chelsea. Spurs won 2-1. Mum & Dad did a bit of gardening at night. Bed: 12:25 a.m.

Sunday 21st

Did most of "My Ideal Home" project. Dad was busy with car & garden, Mum did washing. Grandma came for a few minutes in the afternoon. Brenda's Dad & Maura came in the evening. Ian had a few tears over Canada. Rained at night. Bed: 11:25 p.m.

Monday 22nd

Got very windy in the day. Got letter from Auntie Ruth (Eggleshaw?) to go to Nottingham. Mum decided not to go. Had bad headache all day.

Tuesday 23rd

Came home at dinner time 'cos had a pain in my shoulder. Showers in afternoon. Saw good but sad film at night called "The Blue Angel". Mrs. Hasty came. Bed: 10:20 p.m.

Wednesday 24th

Dad got letter to say he had got the job in Canada. It was a bit doubtful whether he wanted to go & I could have screamed. Got letter from Simon. Did not feel very well at night. Bed: 10:15 p.m.

Thursday 25th

Some football thing was on at night between Celtic & Lisbon. Celtic won 2-1. Top of Pops was shorter. Dad finished filling in the forms for Canada & I posted them. Washed my pen out. Bed: 10:15 p.m.

Friday 26th

Played "Jacks" quite a lot. Got thing from Beatles fan club. Had last lesson with Mrs. Ellingham. Did not do much. Bed: 12 a.m.

Saturday 27th

Drizzled in the morning. Got a Reefer jacket and some "Jacks" from town. Monkees were good. It was sheet lightning at night. Bed: 12:10 a.m.

Sunday 28th

Lightened and thundered about 5 a.m. Played "Jacks" a lot. Dad & Mum painted the kitchen. Grandpa came & so did Brenda's Dad, Maura & Annette. On TV saw Francis Chichester arrive in Plymouth after sailing around the world. Bed: 12:27 a.m.

Monday 29th

Was bored all day. Did not go anywhere except for a walk around the block with Topsy. Dad painted and Mum did the washing. Liz & Dave came at night & Mum & Dad went & had a drink with them. Bed: 12:30 p.m.

Tuesday 30th

Did homework & washed up for Mum. Was rather cold when the sun went in. Dad got the forms for the passports. Nothing much happened. Bed: 10:15 p.m.

Wednesday 31st

Went back to school after Spring Bank holiday. Ian had extra day off. Grandma & Grandpa came at night. Lesley P. went off to Guernsey for a holiday. Bed: 10:35 p.m.

June

Thursday 1st

Mum brought home a picture slide thing home from work on U.S.A. Dad painted kitchen radiator and pipes at night. Nothing much happened. Bed: 10:37 p.m.

Friday 2nd

It was a kind of drizzly fog in the morning. Hot in afternoon. Washed hair. Liz & Dave & Liz's brother came. Talked about C.S.E. a lot at school. Had to tell Miss Harkin what I was going to be. Bed 12:6 a.m.

Saturday 3rd

Went to town. Mum & Dad had passport photos taken. At night Mum & Dad went to dance at Posh Club and to Mrs. Cranswick birthday party. Hair came out nice. Bed 11:35 p.m.

Sunday 4th

Dad did painting. Mum did washing. I did my homework. Ian played with Philip. At night the Bedford's & the Cranswicks came.

Monday 5th

Got letter to say that we were going for medicals. Went to school by myself as Ann's bike had two punctures. My cake went wrong in cookery the filling came out of the middle. It was a hot day. Ian started his first exam. Others went swimming for the first time. Bed: 10:37 p.m.

Tuesday 6th
Was another hot day. Nurse came to look at feet and hair. Got told off by Mrs. Handley in Rounders. Mrs Howitt for French and we saw the Cendrillon play. Bed: 10:25 p.m.

Wednesday 7th
A letter came to confirm Dad's job. Played recorders in prayers. There was writing on the wall in yellow paint about Miss Newborn. Police came and took photos of it. Wasn't allowed to see it. Miss Malster sang in prayers. Bed: 10:46 p.m.

Thursday 8th
Rained a little. Saw Mum's new pendant. Did not do hardly anything in Science. Nothing much happened. Bed: 10:35 p.m.

Friday 9th
Miss Harkin wasn't in school. Wore my school shift for first time this summer. Washed hair. Helped to clean wardrobe out at night to look for birth certificates. Ian went to swimming club for first time. Had a Geog. & R.I. test both were horrible. Bed: 11.10 p.m.

Saturday 10th *ANGELA'S BIRTHDAY*
Was bored all day. Did not go to town. Dad went bowling at night. Mum got some new bedding plants. Posted passport things for Dad. Nothing much happened. Bed: 11:45 p.m.

Sunday 11th
Dad painted hall. Did my homework. Was a cold day. Went to church at night with Mum. Nothing much happened. Bed: 11.0 p.m.

Monday 12th
Two people said my hair looked nice. Mum & Dad went to Dentist in the morning. Got 8 in Cookery for my cheese and veg. flan. Tried to get worm tablets down Topsy but couldn't. Bed: 10:30 p.m.

Tuesday 13th
It was a little misty in morning but a very hot day. Miss Harper called out my name in prayers to be in a fashion parade. Told Miss Wakelin that my dress

wasn't finished. Saw good film at night called "Invitation". Had French in hall & saw "Cendrillon". Bed: 10:45 p.m.

Wednesday 14th
Another very hot day. Did not feel too well. Had my letter signed by Miss Newborn. Had a bath at night. Ian brought some newts home. Bed: 10:22

Thursday 15th
Went to Birmingham but was not very well. Had a good time at the Rotunda and the medical & chest x ray were not as bad as I thought. Hardly had anything to eat that day. Bed: 10:40 p.m.

Friday 16th
Everybody asked me how I had got on. In the afternoon Pauline, Angela & Carol were crying because they had fallen out. Washed hair and dried it quick and it turned out disappointing. Gran & Grandpa came. Bed: 12:10 a.m.

Saturday 17th
Went to town. Had headache. Bought some tights. Dad fixed a new tyre & tube on my bike. Mr. Richardson lost his dog at night and Mum, Ian & I went out looking for it. Could not find it. Bed: 12:15 a.m.

Sunday 18th
Dad & Ian went to the swimming pool at dinner time. I stayed here & did my Geography project. Later after dinner at half 3, Dad, Ian, me & Tops went to Castor Backwaters. We all got nicely suntanned and brown except 'Tops' of course, although my knees, arms & face were all red. Bed 11 p.m.

Monday 19th
Ian stayed at home but was much better at night. Everybody was sunburnt. Hair wasn't right. Got cookery & English results. Did not do much. Bed: 10 45 p.m.

Tuesday 20th
Rained a bit in the morning. Had school sports in afternoon, it was cold. Brenda rode home with me at night. The film was very sad at the end. Bed: 10:45 p.m.

Wednesday 21st
Ian went back to school. Dad got a letter from the passport office. Had new R.I. & English teacher. Did "Pic-a-Pick" competition. Insurance man came at night. Bed: 10.45 p.m.

Thursday 22nd

It was open evening so we did not do hardly anything in the lessons. Brenda went to dentist so I had to bike home by myself at half past 3. Cold sores were healing. Bed: 10:25 p.m.

Friday 23rd

It was a dull day. Cleared up after open evening and saw the play in dress in our Maths lesson. Brenda came at night to do homework with me. Did not get any done. Bed: 11:55 p.m.

Saturday 24th

Brenda came over for five minutes in morning. Went to town & got Brenda some "Jacks", and she came over again at night. We saw last programme of Monkees. Went for a walk & got drenched in rain but tried to shelter under some bushes. Enjoyed myself. Bed: 12:15 a.m.

Sunday 25th

Rained nearly all day terrible. Floods in some places. Jill & John came over in the morning to see if it was true about Canada. Finished "Gone with the Wind". Did my "Ideal Home" project all afternoon. Saw the 2 hour programme of "Our World". Bed: 11:5 p.m.

Monday 26th

Brenda slept at Linda's all night. She came round here in the evening and did her homework. Went round the close with her. [Little Close]

Tuesday 27th

Brenda lost her 'tie-dying', she was very worried. Went to Linda C's. for it on way home but it wasn't there. Went to Brenda's Aunt Thelma's but wasn't there. It was very hot in afternoon. Film was quite good. Bed: 11:00 p.m.

Wednesday 28th

Scabs off my cold sores came off. Brenda came back to fetch her berry [beret] & I walked partly home with her. Dad's passport came. A new teacher in school, Miss Haycock. Bed: 10.45 p.m.

Thursday 29th

Brenda went to dentist in afternoon. Insurance man came again. Did a bit of homework. Brenda came at night and we went for a long walk. Bed: 10:50 p.m.

Friday 30th

Deacon's school boys came round the school. Brenda came at night but we didn't get much homework done. Washed my hair. Dad went out at night & told Gran about Canada. Bed: 11:30 p.m.

July

Saturday 1st

Went to town late in afternoon. Called on Grandma. Brenda came at night. Got some strawberries. Dad told us of the accidents last night. Brenda, 'Tops' and I went in the new bungalows on the new estate. Bed: 11:45 p.m.

Sunday 2nd

Did the rest of my homework and "My Ideal Home". Liz & Dave came at night and took some photos & went to pub with Mum & Dad. Brenda came & showed me her three rosettes. We all went for a walk on the new estate. Bed: 11:5 p.m.

Monday 3rd

Miss Harkin wasn't at school. Anne had cleaned her bike. Had headache at night. Bed: 9:5 p.m.

Tuesday 4th

Miss Harkin was away again today. Brenda & I sat together and watched tennis on the telly. Brenda found her tie-dying & gave me her holiday address. She came round at night. Saw film. Bed: 10:45 p.m.

Wednesday 5th

Mrs. Burt's birthday and we gave her some roses and a card. Miss Harkin came back. Got a postcard from Barbara in Yarmouth. Brenda didn't come here at night. Details about the caravan came. Bed: 10:15 p.m.

Thursday 6th

Last day for some people who go on holiday. Brenda rode home with me for last time and she bought me an ice lolly. Got our reports. School ended at half past 3. Bed: 11:25 p.m.

Friday 7th

Went to All England Sports in morning. Met Helen & Valerie Palmer there. Had lunch there. Then went & got Ian's hipsters. It was very hot and tiring. Mum got me some hairspray & Dad went & had his vaccinations. Washed hair & Jill, John & David came at night. Hair was terrible. Bed: 11.55 p.m.

Saturday 8th

Sports were on for another day but never saw them. Gran & Grandpa came for five minutes then Mum & Dad went to a dance. Ian & I played ball with apples for about 2 hours outside. Bed: 12.5 a.m.

Sunday 9th

Played out in the garden. Did homework & did a little to my "Coffee" project. First of all Graham, Auntie Sheila & Uncle Colin came. Then Brenda's Dad, Maura and Annette came. Lastly Grandma & Grandpa. Quite a hot day. Bed: 10:40 p.m.

Monday 10th

Lesley was on holiday. Barbara came back. Was a very hot day. Made 'scotch eggs' in cookery. Went with Ian to get hair cut but didn't. So we all waited for Mum. Had headache at night. Bed: 10:25 p.m.

Tuesday 11th

Was another very hot day. In Games all we had was rounders. Grandpa came at night. Saw film. Bed: 10:35 p.m.

Wednesday 12th

Another very hot day. Learned where we were going to be next term and our new form mistresses. Did a lot of sewing at night. Gran & Grandpa came. Bed: 10:45 p.m.

Thursday 13th

Heard that Miss Harkin was leaving. Diane Donshak got awarded with a record player & tennis players got awarded in Assembly by education officer. Did not do much in lessons. Got my dress passed finally when holes were punched in belt. Anne had puncture and was away at her sister's in the afternoon. Bed: 10:50 p.m.

Friday 14th
Last day and everybody was signing autograph books. Gave Miss Harkin chocolates and flowers. Betty's group put on a concert for Miss Harkin which was very good. Moved in Room 19 but Miss Roberts was downstairs with the leavers. Started packing at night. Bed: 11.45 p.m.

Saturday 15th
Arrived safely. Had a job finding caravan. Did not like the site at first. Saw California Cliffs at night. Rained a bit when we first arrived.

Sunday 16th
Went into Yarmouth for the day. Took photos down at River Yare with all the ships. Had dinner there. Quite a hot day. Saw the aquarium. Dad, Ian and I went to the beach & played ball. Forgot to write Diary for two days.

Monday 17th
Spent all day down on California beach. Got very sunburnt. It said on the radio that it had been the hottest day ever in East Anglia it was 84 degrees F. Came to caravan for dinner. Bought some sunglasses.

Tuesday 18th
Went into Yarmouth. Saw Brenda's caravan site South Denes. Had dinner at Yarmouth. Went on California beach at night. Ian bought a kite. A gypsy came round and told mum her fortune in morning.

Wednesday 19th
Went on beach most of day. Had dinner come tea at Yarmouth. Got caught on the Britannia pier when it rained. Bought a sombrero hat. Ian bought a furry spider. Saw two people Mum & Dad knew. Mum went to a palmist. Lightened a bit & Dad and Ian went to watch it over the cliff. Very cold at night.

Thursday 20th
Stayed at home with Mum all the day while Dad & Ian went on the beach. Bought some things at shops. At night went to see Morecombe & Wise at the ABC theatre.

Friday 21st
It was Dad's birthday. We went into Yarmouth and bought some presents. A change in the weather it was dull & cold. Spent afternoon packing.

Saturday 22nd
Had a good journey back except for the split tyre & the getting lost in Cambridge. Bought a case from green shield stamps. Grandpa & Grandma were waiting for us when we arrived home. Fetched Topsy from kennels. Liz & Dave came.

Sunday 23rd

Felt rotten with my cold. Had a bath and washed my hair. Liz & Dave came at night and took the van. Grandma & Grandpa came. Mum & Dad went to pub with Liz & Dave. Bed: 1.15 a.m.

Monday 24th

Did not do much all day. Dad went back to work. Phoned up Brenda at night and had a long chat. Ann F. came at night and I gave her the gonk egg cup present. Bed: 11:15 p.m.

Tuesday 25th

Did not do much. Played games with Ian on table. Careers, Battleships and Ball-bearings when Dad came home. Bed: 11.55 p.m.

Wednesday 26th

Mum went to town in morning & got an appointment with the chiropodist for me. Just played games with Ian and tidied my bedroom. Gran & Grandpa came at night. Bed: 12:5 a.m.

Thursday 27th

Had a real bad headache all day. Brenda did not come. Wrote a long letter to Paulyn [Jones, penfriend at 4 Hazel Grove, Horfield, Bristol] in afternoon. Rained a lot in evening and at night. Ian didn't go fishing with Philip. Dad bathed Topsy because she smelt. Bed: 12:5 a.m.

Friday 28th

Had a bath in afternoon. Nothing else much happened. Phoned Brenda up at night but she was not there. Bed: 12:15 a.m.

Saturday 29th

Went to town in morning. Went to chiropodist with my verruca come wart. The lady treated it with acid. Gran & Grandpa came when got home. after Mum had gotten her groceries Bill & Smudge came with Bill's parents. Phoned Brenda up. Bed: 12:25 a.m.

Sunday 30th

Woke up at half past eleven. Grandma & Grandpa came on their way to Aunt Violet's. They were just leaving when Mr & Mrs Cranswick & Sandra came. Dad came home from work at quarter past 10. Bed: 12:40 a.m.

Monday 31st

Had a bad headache all day. Dad went up town on his bike and got his air ticket. Mum started back at work. Washed hair. Bed: 10:55 p.m.

August

Tuesday 1st
Had another bad headache all day. Stayed in. Mr. Richardson died. Saw a very good film called "The Mortal Storm" with James Stewart & Margaret Sullivan.

Wednesday 2nd
Got up very late. Took Mark Canham out in his pram in the afternoon. Had letter from Auntie Ruth & Auntie Cath. Said that Uncle Angus, Uncle Kenneth and Shonagh were coming down at weekend. Gran & Grandpa came. Bed: 10.45 p.m.

Thursday 3rd
Dave came and took Sandy to the vet. He had to be put to sleep. Mum sent a telegram to tell Uncle Angus not to come. Mr. Adie came in the afternoon. Dad's last night at Perkins. Bed: 11:5 p.m.

Friday 4th
Dad brought home his travelling clock present from work. He went to town in the afternoon. I did not do much. Bed: 11:15 p.m.

Saturday 5th
We all went up town including Dad on the bus. The chiropodist removed a lot of my veruca, it was all white. Dad bought a new case and he went bowling at night. Bed: 12:55 a.m.

Sunday 6th
Dad cemented a path in front of the big window. Ann F. came across and gave me a calendar present. Ian was making his new aeroplane at night. Bed: 12.30 a.m.

Monday 7th
Got up late. Dad went to Barclay's bank & got his Canadian dollars. He was painting all day at home. Ian was making his aeroplane. I read a lot more of "Frenchman's Creek". Dave came at night and then Gran & Grandpa. Bed: 12:10 a.m.

Tuesday 8th
Read "Frenchman's Creek" and finished it. Washed hair and set it to flick up. Did not turn out all that good. At night Liz & Dave came and they all went to the pub & left us at home with thunder & lightning. Just after they left the two Mr. Campbell's came. Bed: 1.5 a.m.

Wednesday 9th

Dad & Ian went up town in the afternoon. Dad did the packing & we got a 'Good Luck' telegram from Scotland. Ian was very sick & had a headache in the evening. Grace & Chick Hasty came and then Liz & Dave with their bathroom scales to weigh Dad's luggage. Bed: 11:35 p.m.

Thursday 10th

It was a hectic day. Dad & Ian went to Perkins in Grandpa's car. Mum, Gran & I cleaned up the house. We all went to station in Grandpa's car except Grandma. Saw Dad off. Came home & had tea. Bad thunderstorms through the day. Bed: 11.15 p.m.

Friday 11th

Mum was in at work all day. Dad flew to Canada at 11 a.m. I cleaned up my bedroom a bit. It was thunder and showers on & off all day. Had a bath at night & got my toe soaking wet. Bed: 11:50 p.m.

Saturday 12th

Got a telegram from Dad. Went up town & the chiropodist cut out all of my verruca. It was a dull dull day and cold. Mum lit the central heating. Went to Library & got book called "My Cousin Rachel". I found out that I had seen the film. Bed: 11 p.m.

Sunday 13th

Saw "This Man Craig" after dreaming about it the previous night. Grandma came & left all of Grandpa's birthday cards by mistake. Bed: 11.15 p.m.

Monday 14th

Did a little of my project. Mum was at work full time. Mr. Canham came about the kettle. Heard Radio London close down at 3 o'clock (pm) Bed: 12:10 a.m.

Tuesday 15th

Woke up at 5 to 12. Read all morning papers. Grandpa came. Did some of my project. At night Jill, John, Angela and David came. Bed: 11.30 p.m.

Wednesday 16th

Did not do much at all. Took plaster off my verruca. Found my "Jack" ball or rather Ian did. Bed: 11:35 p.m.

Thursday 17th

Washed my hair, came out alright. Got first two letters from Dad in the morning. Nothing much happened. I was bored. Bed 11:50 p.m.

Friday 18th

Got up late. Didn't do much. Phoned Brenda up and told her all the news.
Bed: 12:15 a.m.

Saturday 19th

Didn't go to town. Spent most of day helping to polish furniture. Watched
Peterborough on "Carnival time". Bed: 12:15 a.m.

Sunday 20th

Brenda & Linda came for a minute when I had just woken up. Spent morning
clearing bedroom for Brenda coming to stay. Was sick in afternoon. Auntie
Sheila, Uncle Colin & Sharon came & had tea. Later Gran & Grandpa came.
Bed: 12:15 a.m.

Monday 21st

Cleaned out Ian's bedroom. Brenda came at night to stay. Then Grandma,
Grandpa, Aunt Violet & Mrs. Coles came, it was a hot day. Bed: 11:45 p.m.

Tuesday 22nd

Brenda & I took Mark Canham for a walk. It was a very hot day. Afterwards
we did our projects. Jill, John & David came at night. Then Brenda & I took
Topsy for a walk. Bed: 12:35 a.m.

Wednesday 23rd

It was another very hot day. Had another letter from Dad. Mum wrote one
off. Had no luck with taking any babies out. Gran & Grandpa came at night.
Bed: 12:50 a.m.

Thursday 24th

We took Mark out. When we got back I washed my hair then we did more to
our "Ideal Homes" projects. Grandpa came at night. Bed: 1.20 a.m.

Friday 25th

Got up very late. After breakfast we took Mark out. Then Brenda covered
her books and cleared her things up. Mum went to town & when she came
home Brenda's Dad came to fetch Brenda. Bed: 12:40 a.m.

Saturday 26th

Had bath in morning. Letter came from penpal Phyllis to say that she
received my parcel. Cleaned my bedroom up. Bed: 12:15 a.m.

Sunday 27th

Mr. Allen called in the morning about Dad's letters. Watched the telly in
afternoon. Mum & I went to church at night. Then Grandpa came. Bed:
11:50 p.m.

Monday 28th
Had tummy ache bad all day. Only had a cheese butty to eat. Grandma & Grandpa came at night. It was Bank August Monday. Bed: 10:55 p.m.

Tuesday 29th *IAN'S BIRTHDAY*
It was Ian's birthday and he got 4 cards. Got a letter from Dad with some housing brochures. They were too dear. Grandpa came in afternoon. Bed: 11:30 p.m.

Wednesday 30th
No letter from Dad came about the money and Mum has a feeling that he will come home at the weekend. Had a bad headache. Bed: 11:45 p.m.

Thursday 31st
Had a headache. Did Geog. project. Phoned Brenda but she couldn't come to Pictures. At night Grandpa came and then Roselyn, Jim & Sean. Bed 11.40 p.m.

September

Friday 1st
Washed hair & had a bath. Rained in the evening. At night Jill, John, David & Angela Kendle [Mum's cousin Jill, 49 Malvern Road, Gunthorpe, Peterborough] *came.*

Saturday 2nd
Got Canadian 'Bramalea' newspaper from Dad. Went up town & did all school shopping. Stayed & watched Morecombe & Wise at Odeon. Mum was tired out & went to bed early. I did my project & Ian drew. Bed: 12:10 a.m.

Sunday 3rd
Finished both of my projects off. It was a windy & rainy day. Gran & Grandpa came. Nothing much happened. Bed: 12:40 a.m.

Monday 4th
It was my last day of freedom. A letter from Dad came in morning written in gold ink. Cleaned my bike. Janet Wright came at night. Bed: 10:10 p.m.

Tuesday 5th
Went back to school today. Wasn't too bad but was very windy. Anne Taylor was not at school. Rained as well. Phoned Cotton's TV for Ann F., Mr. & Mrs. Bedford and Vicki. Bed: 11.00 p.m.

Wednesday 6th

Was not so windy. Got a new bike rack. Nothing much happened. Bed: 10:25 p.m.

Thursday 7th

Had Art with Mr. Scott. Ian went back to school. Nothing much happened. Bed: 10:30 p.m.

Friday 8th

Some girls pushed me over coming in after break. Brenda came home with me to do her homework. Got two postcards from Dad of Niagara Falls. Washed hair & had a bath. Bed: 11:20 p.m.

Saturday 9th

Went to town but first to get Ian's hair cut at Nicky's. Got some pink material for a skirt. Sent 14/- off to get a new paper dress. Saw Brenda in town. Got a map of Toronto from Dad and a postcard from Anne in Hythe. Bed: 11:30 p.m.

Sunday 10th

Didn't have much homework. At night Uncle Angus, Auntie Kathy and their friends Andy & Sheena came on their way to Germany for the night unexpected. Then came Gran & Grandpa but before them Mr. & Mrs. Cranswick & Sandra. Bed: 10:15 p.m.

Monday 11th

Anne had come back from her holidays but stayed at home 'cos she got home late. Got a nice long letter from Dad. Brenda's Dad & Maura came at night to ask if Brenda could stay here one night 'cos of her brother. Bed: 10:55

Tuesday 12th

Anne came back. Had my hair in bunches. Brenda was supposed to come and stay the night but didn't. Bed: 10.5 p.m.

Wednesday 13th

Anne gave us her rock. Brenda came home with me and stayed the night. We had a lot of homework. Bed: 10: 35 p.m.

Thursday 14th

Mrs. Burt got mad with us in Maths. Drizzled all day. Nothing much happened. Bed: 9:55 p.m.

Friday 15th

Ann F. & Lesley P. went to a dance. Mum went to town at night and got some medicine for my tum. Bed: 10:40 p.m.

Saturday 16th

Had a bath & washed my hair. Tidied my bedroom a bit. Nothing much happened. Bed: 11:30 p.m.

Sunday 17th

Got up rather early and it was foggy. Did my homework but could not find a brown crayon. Gran & Grandpa came. Went to church where they gave out Sunday School certificates. Bed: 10:35 p.m.

Monday 18th

Made fish cakes with Miss West. Brenda became a prefect. Nothing much happened. Bed: 10:00 p.m.

Tuesday 19th

Rained nearly all day & was very cold. Had our first proper game of hockey. Had first TV Careers. Had a bad headache all day. Bed: 10:02 p.m.

Wednesday 20th

It was a cold wind. They launched Queen Elizabeth II today & some girls got to see it on telly. Had our first history TV. Bed: 10:30 p.m.

Thursday 21st

Nothing much happened. Mum wrote to Dad in Canada telling him to come home. Cut out my skirt pattern at night. Bed: 10:40 p.m.

Friday 22nd

Started on my skirt at school. Brenda came to stay the night & did my hair lovely. Liz & Dave came. Bed: 12:30 a.m.

Saturday 23rd

Brenda biked home at dinner time. I biked a little way with her. Was a dull day & drizzled at times. Cleaned my bedroom out & had a bath. Bed: 10:55 p.m.

Sunday 24th

Mum was ill in bed all day with a migraine attack. Did some of the housework and made an apple crumble. Gran & Grandpa came. Bed: 10:30 p.m.

Monday 25th
Had a slight cold. Nothing much happened. Bed: 9:55 p.m.

Tuesday 26th
It was a hot and cold day. Central heating was turned on in school. Had two students for hockey. Saw good programme at night about the Queen Mary. Bed: 10:55 p.m.

Wednesday 27th
Had a very bad stomach ache. Got letter, cheque & photo's from Dad. Bed: 10: 25 p.m.

Thursday 28th
Fell out with Anne T. Nothing much happened. Bed: 10: 55 p.m.

Friday 29th
Hem came down at dinner time. Brenda came & did my hair. Bed: 1 a.m.

Saturday 30th
It was strong head wind for Brenda to go home in. Mum was at work in the morning and got her new black and white suit. Heard that Cliff Richards is to sing in the Eurovision song contest. Monkees started again & taped 2 songs. Bed: 11:50 p.m.

October

Sunday 1st
Was doing "My Ideal Home" from morning till night trying to finish it. Mum's work friend Patricia Coles & her boyfriend Stuart came. Then Mr. & Mrs. Bedford & Vicky & then John, Jill, Angela & David. Bed: 10:45 p.m.

Monday 2nd
Made spaghetti bolognese in Cookery. Ian was ill with cold so stayed home all day. Nurse was in school but I don't know what for. Bed: 10:30 p.m.

Tuesday 3rd
It was a very windy day. Got letter from McDonald's about kilt - too expensive. Saw film about Reynard's Mill, Hong Kong last lesson. It was sad. Bed: 10.00 p.m.

Wednesday 4th
Had a letter from Dad saying he had put his wages away to come home. Brenda lost our recorders in the Maths room. Bed: 10:30 p.m.

Thursday 5th

Went to Baker Perkins offices in afternoon it was good. Nothing much happened. Bed: 10:45 p.m.

Friday 6th

Had to do curtains in sewing 'cos Miss Harper wasn't there. Brenda came and did my hair lovely with her hair dryer. Saw very good "Boy meets Girl" story called "Long Hot Summer". It was the last one with a Norfolk boy in. Bed: 12:40 a.m.

Saturday 7th

Mum & Ian went to get Ian's hair cut. Found my "Wuthering Heights". Brenda went early cursing because it was windy. Bed: 11:15 p.m.

Sunday 8th

Didn't have much homework. In morning Mr. & Mrs. Bedford & Vicky came & Mr. Bedford mended Mum's puncture. I made some cheese scones, then Gran & Grandpa came. Had big spider on me! Bed: 10:50 p.m.

Monday 9th

Had quite a lot of Maths homework. Nothing much happened. Bed: 11.00 p.m.
Bed: 11.00 p.m.

Tuesday 10th

Didn't have hockey 'cos it rained all day. Nothing much happened. Bed: 10:20 p.m.

Wednesday 11th

Rained all day again. Was asked to do prefect duty tomorrow by gate at dinner time. Miss Roberts was not there. Letter from Dad at night saying he was coming home. Bed: 10: 50 p.m.

Thursday 12th

Ann Foster went to see "She stoops to Conquer" at Northampton. So rode home by myself. Was prefect for the day & stood at main gate. A cablegram came from Dad saying that he was at Uncle Jim's in New York & would be coming home soon. Bed: 10:37 p.m.

Friday 13th

It was a Friday the 13th. My paper dress came. Brenda came & did my hair different it turned out okay but took ages to dry. Could not write my diary 'cos there was a big spider in bedroom. Bed: 12:45 a.m. (about).

Saturday 14th

Went partly home with Brenda and it rained. It was a rainy and windy day. Got all my homework done. Monkees was quite good and I taped 1 song. Bed: 20.00 a.m. Dad came home.

Sunday 15th

First Grandma & Grandpa came. Then Mr. & Mrs. Bedford and Vicky. They were all shocked to see Dad. Bed: 10:25 p.m.

Monday 16th

It was bitter cold and rained all afternoon. Dad went to town and Grandpa brought him back. He stayed for tea with my Beef Casserole, then they went to see Dad's old foreman. Bed: 10: 30 p.m.

Tuesday 17th

Got our medical forms. Was very windy and cold in morning. Mum went to Ear hospital & town. Dad was still on the dole since yesterday. Bed: 10:35 p.m.

Wednesday 18th

Was still very cold. Had a lot of homework. Anne & Brenda went to Cathedral at night for concert & to sell programmes. Liz & Dave came. Bed: 10:25 p.m.

Thursday 19th

Had harvest festival and I took a tin of pilchards and some onions. Was still very cold. Ian's viewer came. Gym was horrible with Miss Jessop but was last lesson. Bed: 10:10p.m.

Friday 20th

Broke up for half term. Heard spooky story about Room A. Brenda could not come 'cos she was helping her Dad. Had a bath & washed my own hair. While I was in bath, Mr. & Mrs. Hasty & Linda came. Bed: 11:50 p.m.

Saturday 21st

Bought some whisky, beer & 7 Up for Dad. Made an orange meringue pie. Only saw beginning of Monkees 'cos Brenda's Dad, Maura, Annette & Brenda came. Bed: 12:5 a.m.

Sunday 22nd

Was fed up. Grandpa came. At night Liz & Dave came and we all had a drink. Bed: 12:10 a.m.

Monday 23rd

Brenda came. In morning I was sick and had stomach ache. We took Mark out. At night my stomach hurt again. Then Bill MacFarlane came. Bed: 11: 30 p.m.

Tuesday 24th

Got some tomatoes from the nursery for Mum in morning. Made Spaghetti Bolognese for tea. Wrote two letters. Got cramp. Bed 11:35 p.m.

Wednesday 25th

Mr. Crowson came in morning. Phoned Brenda up about my homework. I had forgotten my General Notebook. It was a windy day. Bed: 11:55 p.m.

Thursday 26th

Another very windy day. Got up late in a bad mood. Phoned Brenda and had a long chat. Played cards with Ian. Mum had a bad head & went to bed early. Bed: 11:50 p.m.

Friday 27th

Phoned Brenda up in morning. Rained nearly all day. Washed hair and had a bath. Hair came out terrible. Dad went to see Burdette's factory for a job. Bed: 11:50 p.m.

Saturday 28th

Felt real depressed in morning. Mum was ill in bed. Monkees good, taped a song. It rained. Had cramp at night. Phoned Brenda but she could not come. Bed: 11:45 p.m. Put clocks back.

Sunday 29th

The last day of half term. The Bedfords came in the morning, Mum & I had to dash out & get plant for Mrs. Bedford's birthday (day before). Then Carol Gifford & friend came. Then Gran & Grandpa. Made a Beef Casserole.

Monday 30th

Made Christmas cake at school. It was okay till I baked it then it burnt. Bed: 10:30 p.m.

Tuesday 31st *HALLOWEEN*

It was a windy and rainy day, got soaked at dinner time.. Supposed to be first day of medicals but doctor was ill. Broke back light on my bike. Bed: 10:35 p.m.

November

Wednesday 1st

It was another rainy day. Had my pre-medical. Others had their medical with man doctor. Saw play called "Pitchi Poi" in the "Largest theatre in the World". Bed: 10:50 p.m.

Thursday 2nd

It was another wet day. Mum & Ian got the fireworks. Big ring on cooker went. Played Table tennis in Gym. Bed: 10:30 p.m.

Friday 3rd

Yet another wet day. Mary Holman hit me so Dad & I went to the house and got it sorted out. Washed hair. Came out OK. Jill & John came, when I had gone to bed. Bed: 11.30 p.m.

Saturday 4th

It was Mum's 17th wedding anniversary & Guy Fawkes night. Made my second Christmas cake, it turned out OK. My hair was nice. Bedford's supposed to come but didn't turn up. Rained. Bed 11:20 p.m.

Sunday 5th

Had a bad headache nearly all day. The Bedfords came. Had quite a bit of homework to do. Bed: 10:30 p.m.

Monday 6th

Made sausage rolls in Cookery. Heard the "Sound of Music" in Music. Phoned Brenda up to give her bit of history, for test. Let off rest of fireworks. Bed: 10:40 p.m.

Tuesday 7th

The first frost (I think). Some of our class had medicals. Got new book in English called "Anne Frank's diary". It is quite good. Did not have Careers TV because of a memorial service. Bed: 11:50 p.m.

Wednesday 8th

Was a very foggy day. Got let out of school at 10 to 4. Brenda & Anne T. had their medicals. Had a bath. Bed: 10:5 p.m.

Thursday 9th

Had my medical. It was OK. Dad got letter to say job in Burdette's was taken. Some classes went to see Julius Caesar at Pictures. Miss Roberts was out for day. Played Badminton in Gym. It was better than Table tennis. Bed: 10:35 p.m.

Friday 10th

Mrs. Burt got mad about Cornerstone's in Maths. Burnt myself on cooker. Bed: 10:15 p.m.

Saturday 11th

Helped Mum clean up. Made some sausage rolls. Dad & Ian went to Nicky's for haircut. Monkees were not on because of programme to do with Poppy day. Brenda's Dad & Maura came at night to tell us of christening tomorrow. Said I was to be Godmother. Bed:11:20 p.m.

Sunday 12th

It was Annette's Christening. There were two other christenings at the same time. Didn't have to say anything on my own. Had tea afterwards. Then Brenda's Auntie & Uncle & two cousins Susan & David Piccaver came. Brenda's Dad brought us & took us home at 8 o'clock. Bed: 10:25 p.m.

Monday 13th

Made Eccles cakes in cookery. Ann F. told me about her being in the Miss Eye contest as one of the attendants. Dad went to Pistol Club at night. Bed: 10:30 p.m.

Tuesday 14th

Rest of people had their medicals. Brenda was runner & then they ended. Did not have Careers on TV 'cos it was only about building. Had hockey. Heard about an Art exhibition we were going to. Bed:

Wednesday 15th

Dad got letter from Hotpoint about job he didn't get. School TV went wrong. Didn't watch telly for 2nd night 'cos of homework. John Kendle came to see Dad in afternoon. Bed: 10:40 p.m.

Thursday 16th

Had my interview with Miss Blake. Everything went OK. In afternoon went to see Art Exhibition. Did not stay long. Saw Miss World at night. Miss Peru won. Bed: 10:35 p.m.

Friday 17th

Said that I would read with Susan Bools on stage. New teacher called Miss Smith. I did not carry Brenda's books upstairs. Mum went to town at night & got my cake board. Washed hair had bath. Bed: 10:40 p.m.

Saturday 18th

Saw Monkees with new hairstyles. It was foggy at night. Mum & Dad went to Posh Club dance. Had bad cough. Did my homework & read a lot of "Anne Frank's Diary". Bed: 12:40 a.m.

Sunday 19th

Still had bad cough. Stomach ache in afternoon. Made Casserole of Beef. First Chick Hasty came, then Mr. & Mrs. Bedford & Vicki. At night Mr. & Mrs. Abbott came. Wrote letter to pen pal Sue Forster. Saw little of "Royal Performance Show." Bed: 10:45 p.m.

Monday 20th

Marzipanned my cake, it wasn't all that good. Didn't have very bad stomach ache. Had my bad cough. Dad met me out of school. Was a dull day. Had arguments at night about politics. Bed: 10:30 p.m.

Tuesday 21st

Stayed away from school with my bad cough. Grandpa wondered why I hadn't been there & came round. In afternoon had croak in my voice. By night I could hardly speak and got some horrible brown medicine. Tried out my menthol crystals. Bed: 9:55 p.m.

Wednesday 22nd

My voice was better & so was my cough a bit. Sent Brenda a letter & she sent me one back at night with my history homework which I did. Then I wrote her another letter. Dad had medical at Perkins. Bed:11:00 p.m.

Thursday 23rd

Cough was a little better. Mum did washing. Dad went to see Mr. Ruff. Did my project. John Kendle came at night & he went with Dad to have a look at some cars. Bed: 10:35 p.m.

Friday 24th

Dad went to town & to Mr. Allan's. My cough & cold & bad head came on & I finally got some Meggezones. Had bath & washed my hair. Got letter from Brenda. Read quite a bit of "The Moonstone" book which Brenda sent yesterday. Bed 12:15 a.m.

Saturday 25th

Was very ill in bed & didn't write my Diary. Felt real rough & had a very bad headache & cold. Mum & Ian went up town in afternoon.

Sunday 26th

Felt better and got up. Mum did all the cooking. Got cleaned up. Grandpa came. Nothing much happened. Bed: 10.00 p.m.

Monday 27th

Went back to school although I still had a bad cold. I put the icing on my cake. It didn't turn out very special. Dad started work at Perkins. Bed: 10:45 p.m.

Tuesday 28th

Drizzled in the morning and I got let off hockey in the afternoon with a note. Went to Library. Brenda was sucking cough sweets all morning & felt sick in afternoon. Ann F. got some lights for her bike. Bed: 10:30 p.m.

Wednesday 29th

It was Grandma's birthday & she got 15 cards. Made some bacteria in science. Nothing much happened. Bed: 10:25 p.m.

Thursday 30th

Mr. Barley & Mrs. Harrison were away. Varnished my carrier bag in art. Nothing much happened. Bed: 11:45 p.m.

December

Friday 1st

Got no homework for weekend. Washed hair & had bath. Hair wasn't all that good. Brenda had to rush from school to go to party at the Saunders. Bed: 11:25 p.m.

Saturday 2nd

Had headache Dad was at work all day. Mum got things for trimmings. Wrote my Christmas cards. Taped some of Monkees songs. Saw film about a man almost jumping off a ledge. Bed: 12:15 a.m.

Sunday 3rd

Made the "stew" again. Mr. & Mrs. Bedford & Vicki came. Went to church. Liz & Dave came at night. Bed: 10:20 p.m.

Monday 4th

Finished off my Christmas cake with yellow piping. The Dress rehearsal for "Bells of Brugge" was on, so did not have many teachers for lessons. Jill & John, Angela & David came at night. Bed: 10:30 p.m.

Wednesday 6th

It was a very cold day & heard of snow in places. Had science test & I got the lowest marks. Put chairs out for "Bells of Bruges" in music & let out at half past 3. Bed: 10:40 p.m.

Thursday 7th

It was another very very cold day. Went to "Bells of Bruges" at night. Biked to Lesley's & went in Lesley's Dad's car. Mr. Whiting brought us home & it was very late so left bikes at Lesleys. Bed: 11:10 p.m.

Friday 8th

It was still very very cold. All we did in needlework was to put costumes away. Had a very cold netball lesson. Used my hair dryer for the first time. My hair went all springy but nice. Bed: 10:55 p.m.

Saturday 9th

My hair was nice. Made trimmings & hung them up & decorated the Christmas tree. Had the first lot of snow. Went round town & got the Christmas presents. It was all slushy & I nearly slipped over. Mum got some new boots. At night I made a Victoria Sandwich & iced it. Bed: 11:45 p.m.

Sunday 10th

Snowed again in the morning. Couldn't do my Maths construction homework. Wrapped up Christmas presents. In the afternoon Auntie Lucy, Auntie Joyce & all the Greens [from Holbeach Drove] came & brought Christmas presents. Bed: 11:5 p.m.

Monday 11th

The roads to school were clear of snow. My hair was lovely in the morning & got lots of compliments. Rained in afternoon & night so hair spoilt. Got T.C.P. ointment all over my hands & legs 'cos sore. Bed: 10:20 p.m.

Tuesday 12th

It had all thawed out. In morning in hymn practice we did our descants for carols at the cathedral. It wasn't very good. Last lesson we had talk by a sergeant about road safety. Bed: 10:40 p.m.

Wednesday 13th

Went to cathedral in the afternoon. Sat in front of choir stalls. Eastholm sang the descant with us. I don't know whether we did bad or good. We were the first there & had to be back early from dinner. Dad's tool box had come & Mum's bathroom set. Bed: 10:15 p.m.

Thursday 14th

In afternoon we had badminton. Mr. Scott had gone to a funeral in art. Mum got a pass out half an hour earlier and went to party with Jill. Bed: 10:10 p.m.

Friday 15th

Was a little late in morning. Mum came up to see cake display & Brenda was one of the winners. Anne T. took hers home at dinner time by taxi & had the afternoon off. Grandpa took my cake home for me. Washed my hair & had a bath. Bed: 11:40 p.m.

Saturday 16th

Had stomach ache all day. Finished "The Moonstone". Hung up Christmas cards. Dad & Ian went to barbers. Wrote out some cards. At night Dad went to a man about the watches & took mine. Did my project. Ian had cold. Mum did washing. Bed: 11:15 p.m.

Sunday 17th

Made Sunday dinner, then Mr. & Mrs. Bedford & Vicki came. When they were going, the Salvation Army Band were round & Grandpa & Grandma came. Got dinner when they went. Then made 4 Russian meat pies. Saw carol service on telly. Bed: 10:15 p.m.

Monday 18th

Anne was not at school. In cookery we made a pudding, then cleaned the cookers & cleared everything up. Anne had bad cold & all her family were in bed. Played "bingo" game in Maths. Gave out all my presents. Bed: 10:25 p.m.

Tuesday 19th

Did not do much all day. Had hockey in afternoon, it was freezing. Choir people were at St. Barnabas for practise for tonight. Bed: 10:55 p.m.

Wednesday 20th

Did not do much in morning. Stayed in form rooms in afternoon. Gave out Christmas cards, was not too successful for me. Got present from Auntie Sheila & co. at Grandma's at dinner time. Was the worst frosty day. Broke up from school for Christmas. Bed: 10:55 p.m.

Thursday 21st

Did mostly housework & games today. Had a bath. Dad got staff job. Brenda, Maura, Brenda's Dad & Annette came for a few minutes. Watched a programme about Canada on telly. Bed: 11:45 p.m.

Friday 22nd

Washed hair in morning. Mum did her shopping at Spitz shop in the High Street & got some drink. Had my hair in pony tail for town. Got rest of Christmas shopping. Was worn out. Maura & Brenda's Dad came for a few minutes. Bed: 10:25 p.m.

Saturday 23rd

Tidied up my bedroom & ottoman. Was tired after that & did nothing else. At night Grandma & Grandpa came, then they took Mum & Dad to the Posh Club. Monkees Christmas show was good if only I could have heard it. Bed: 11:45 p.m.

Sunday 24th

Made some mince pies. At night after watching "David Copperfield" Bill & Smudge came with Sharon's present. Saw their new puppy "Rusty". At night saw very good film all about Gladys Aylward. The film was very good but I had watched too much telly. Bed: 12:15 a.m.

Monday 25th

Got up at 9 o'clock & opened presents. Ian had been up since 8 o'clock. At one o'clock Gran & Grandpa came. Was argument about Grandpa & pub. Aunt Violet didn't come 'cos scared of burglars at her house. Went over to Auntie Sheila's with presents. After dinner watched tv, played cards, had tea and then played Bingo. Dad had a bad cold. Bed: 12:15 a.m.

Tuesday 26th

Got up in a bad & sad mood. Before I could get breakfast, Mr. & Mrs. Bedford & Vicki came. Saw films on telly. At night Gran & Grandpa came for 10 mins. Afterwards saw "Magical Mystery Tour" by Beatles. It was queer. Bed: 12:15 a.m.

Wednesday 27th

Got up after midday, did some housework & played draughts. Mum didn't feel too well nor Dad who started his new job. At night Jill, John, Angela & David came & stayed quite late. Mum brought home more chocs from work. Bed: 12:15 a.m.

Thursday 28th

Phoned up Brenda & had quick chat. She wasn't coming over, disappointed. Did some housework. At night saw "Long after summer" again (Oct 6th). It was very good. Bed: 11:45 p.m.

Friday 29th

Made a Victoria sandwich with wells in the middle so that the cake mixture rose evenly. Tried to phone Brenda but so many people at phone box. Finally got through to Maura who said Brenda had gone to her Mum's to stay. Had a bath & washed my hair. Bed: 11:15 p.m.

Saturday 30th

Went to town early. Bought a film for camera 'cos no poly photos. Was cold. At night Dad & Mum went to New Year's Eve dance at Tech. College. Bed: 12:10 a.m.

Sunday 31st

Did bit of cooking in the morning. Phoned up Brenda's Dad & they came down. In evening Jill, John, Angela & David came for tea. After tea Liz & Dave came & then the Bedfords. Liz & Dave left to go to a party. At about 11:15 p.m. they all went. Watched the New Year in on TV a bit. Bed: 12:30 a.m.

14-2-67

JANE EYRE

…..but a day or two afterwards I learned that Miss Temple, on returning to her own room at dawn, had found me laid in a little crib; my face against Helen Burns's shoulder, my arms around her neck. I was asleep, and Helen was - dead.

Charlotte Bronte.

January

Monday 1st

Was Mum's birthday & she got five cards all with Roses on. [Her name was Rosemary] *Saw film on telly called "The 39 steps". Was supposed to go & baby sit for Uncle Colin but Grandpa was ill & could not take me. Dad came home early to tell me, but Mrs. Rome had already come with the phone message. Snowed at night. All had early nights. Bed: 10.25 p.m.*

Tuesday 2nd

Snow all melted away in morning. Did some ironing & revised Maths. Dad took Grandpa into Doctors. At night Mum & I went to pay the coalman's bill. Bed: 11.40 p.m.

Wednesday 3rd

A cold day & did the same as yesterday. Went out and phoned Maura up who said Brenda would be back on Saturday. Next door they had the Eastern Gas. Mum will not have it as she has heard of explosions. Got a headache at night. Mum was in work full-time for a day. Bed: 11.45 p.m.

Thursday 4th

Mum wasn't in work full-time. Did same as yesterday. Peter Tork from the Monkees was on "Top of the Pops". Was bored all day. Bed: 11 p.m.

Friday 5th

Rained all day. Washed hair & had a bath. Hair didn't dry properly. A boring day. Bed: 11.40 p.m.

Saturday 6th

Had letter from Auntie Audrey saying that I was in her Will. Didn't do much but made attempt to tidy my bedroom. Saw thriller on airplane film at night. Bed: 11.30 p.m.

Sunday 7th

Made the stew. Saw two good films on telly. Nothing else happened. Bed: 11.40 p.m.

Monday 8th

Was a boring day. At night had to get ready for bed early. Nothing much happened. Bed: 10:10 p.m.

Tuesday 9th
Went back to school. It snowed awful bad in the night and we had to walk to school [2.5 miles] getting there late. Wasn't a bad first day. At night walked home again but this time it was agony as it was much colder & head wind. In the night there was a terrible rumble. It was a pipe on the garage. Bed: 10.50 p.m.

Wednesday 10th
Talked about exams most of day. Roads were all clear except Hodney Road so biked. Played out in snow at night with Ian. Liz & Dave came.

Thursday 11th
The snow still had not melted. Did our practical cookery exam. Got a birthday card from Jill & John. Bed: 10.40 p.m.

Friday 12th
Went to school & got stomach ache in Needlework. Came home at dinner time in agony. Stayed away all afternoon. Got five [birthday] cards altogether. Adding up Christmas & Birthday money I've got £2.15s. Bed: 10.45 p.m.

Saturday 13th
Washed my hair & had a bath. Got birthday card from Kathy. Cleaned up my bedroom. Dad went bowling at night. Bed: 11.45 p.m.

Sunday 14th
Made a Victoria Sandwich. Saw a film & revised a little. Mum was busy cleaning the house up. At night Auntie Audrey & Uncle Lionel came. Rained the other night & all the snow had melted by morning. Bed: 10.15 p.m.

Monday 15th
It was a very windy day. Hurricanes in places. Got knocked off my bike [by a non-emergency ambulance] and taken to hospital. Got away with bruises & scratches. It was reported in the evening paper. Stayed away from school & missed the first day of exams. Had bad headache. Bed: 10.50 p.m.

Tuesday 16th
Felt washed out. All stiff and bruised all over. Still had headache. Read about me in the paper & had a letter from Miss Newborn. At night Brenda & family came. Bed: 10.45 p.m.

Wednesday 17th
Ian went back to school. Got a "Get well" card from Barbara, Anne & Susan. Felt better than yesterday. Dad brought my bike home at night. Bed 10.45 p.m.

Thursday 18th
Looked at old photos. Kept bumping my bruised elbow & couldn't write my diary at night. Got late Christmas card from Phyllis.

Friday 19th
Arm got better. Was a mild day. Washed my hair & had a bath. Rang Brenda at night but she wasn't there. Bed: 12.5 a.m.

Saturday 20th
Went up town & got a skirt, blouse & cardigan. Was disappointed. Got good books out of Library & Ian got his model V.C.10. Bed: 11.50 p.m.

Sunday 21st
Made the stew, read a lot more of "Octavia". Jill, John & Angela popped in for a minute then went to collect David from a party. Bed: 10.30 p.m.

Monday 22nd
Went back to school & got a lot of "How are you's". Miss Roberts wasn't there in morning nor Anne T. 'cos she had a sceptic thumb. Exams were on in some rooms. Went to see in the afternoon "Taming of the Shrew", was good. Brenda came home with me 'cos had no lights & stayed night. Bed: 11.00 p.m.

Tuesday 23rd
Brenda did my hair up for me. Got off hockey with my bruises. Finished off "Octavia". Most people like my hair. Talked about the exams in two lessons. It was a cold day. Bed: 10.30 p.m.

Wednesday 24th
Ann F. told me of her prospects of going to Sweden. Had maths in Art room 'cos of exams. Read the books "Modern Living" in Science. Dad got a film for the editor thing. Anne T. was away in the afternoon 'cos her mum had gone to a funeral. Bed: 11.00 p.m.

Thursday 25th
Made bread in cookery. Heard about girls being off with German Measles. Nothing much happened. Bed: 10.15 p.m.

Friday 26th
It wasn't too cold. Washed hair and had a bath at night. Bed: 10.10 p.m.

Saturday 27th

Did a bit of housework through the day. Ian had his hair cut. Mum & Dad went to Posh club at night. Watched "Invaders" on telly, it was good. Bed: 12.30 a.m.

Sunday 28th

Made the stew for tomorrow's tea. Next door they were getting the garage down. Went to Crowland Auntie Audrey & Uncle Lionel Sharpe's for tea. It was good fun & Auntie Audrey had got the "Beatles: Hard Day's Night L.P.". Bed: 10.50 p.m.

Monday 29th

Had good time playing table tennis in Gym. Brenda who had a rotten cold told me about her fun Sunday. Missed Double Maths for the 4th time 'cos had lecture on Oxfam. Mr. Crowson came at night. Ian was ill in bed all day. Bed: 10.10 p.m.

Tuesday 30th

Ian was better. Brenda still had rotten cold & got off hockey, although it wasn't too cold out. Saw Cilla Black's first show & on it saw the Rotunda [Birmingham]. Bed: 10.40 p.m.

Wednesday 31st

Brenda was away with her cold. Heard about having student, Miss Baxter for Maths. Six people away altogether. Had bad stomach ache at night. Ian went to school. Bed: 11.00 p.m.

February

Thursday 1st

Had Mrs. Hall for cookery & had the most hectic lesson yet. Dinner time I rushed to chemist for Cystex tablets rushed to dinner. Rushed back to Anne's & got "Octavia". Rushed to Cilla's & phoned Brenda. Rushed back to school. 7 away today.

Friday 2nd

Brenda came back to school. Played a hot Badminton game. Was disappointed with my library books at night so went out & rang Brenda about going to town but she was out. Washed my hair & had a bath. Bed: 11.15 p.m.

Saturday 3rd

Went to town with Brenda in morning. Very cold and snowed a little. Had a bad headache all day. Did a lot of shopping. Bed: 12.5 a.m.

Sunday 4th

Heard of snow but here it was very windy & raining at night. Went to church. In afternoon saw "Kitty" film, 2nd time. Brenda's Dad, Maura & Annette came for a few minutes. Bed: 10.50 p.m.

Monday 5th

Was slippery in morning & a car skidded right round in front of us while we were riding our bikes to school. Brenda came late 'cos her Dad took her bike accidently. Very cold day & rained at night. Dad phoned up about a caravanette holiday in Cornwall & to Dr. Smith about Grandpa. Had a bad headache. Had double Maths for first time this term. Bed: 10 p.m.

Tuesday 6th

Said my speech in Careers. Was another very cold day. After school Brenda went to have her ears pierced. Mum & I went at night to church to see Vicar's display of old Eye. Caravanette idea too expensive. Bed: 10.55 p.m.

Wednesday 7th

Brenda had had her ears pierced & had to keep bathing them. Lesley S. was crying over a pony that got run over. Had film in science. Could not do my History homework questions & got upset. Bed: 11.15 p.m.

Thursday 8th

Was cold. One of Ian's fishes died. Nothing much happened. Bed: 10.40 p.m.

Friday 9th

Miss Roberts was away. Rained nearly all day. Mum was at Gran's at dinner time. Washed hair & had bath at night. Bed: 12.00 a.m.

Saturday 10th

Had bad stomach ache. Dad & Ian went to town so Mum & I went to see"Dr. Zhivago". We didn't like it & came out at the intermission. Dad went out bowling at Corby with team. Bed: about 1 p.m.

Sunday 11th *BRENDA'S BIRTHDAY.*

Helped clean up house in morning. In afternoon went bowling with Auntie Audrey & Uncle Lionel. It was crowded but got a lane after 20 mins. Came home for tea & played Careers. Bed: 11.30 p.m.

Monday 12th

Was a cold day & drizzled again. Brenda came to school on her new bike. Anne W. had to be taken home 'cos spots (German Measles). Mum went to Gran's at dinner. Brenda showed me all her cards. Dad & I got the Valentine cards ready. Bed: 10.45 p.m.

Tuesday 13th

Thought it was Shrove Tuesday but wasn't, had pancakes anyway. Posted Dad's 4 Valentine's in Central Ave. at dinner time. Anne T. had got German measles & I thought I'd got it. Uncle Roy came to see us at night. Bed: 11.10 p.m.

Wednesday 14th ♡'s day.

Dad got one & so did Mum. Had the photographer & got my photo taken. Roselyn Eagle was very nasty. Had student Miss Baxter to teach us in Maths. Mrs. Burt looked mad when we didn't know anything. Had meat demonstration by Mr. Rayment. Bed: 11.25 p.m.

Thursday 15th

Had a peaceful nice cookery lesson. Ellis Cooper in "Newcomers" died. It was very sad. Wrote away for a french pen friend. Bed: 10.30 p.m.

Friday 16th

Heard about Mumps going around. Brenda was on prefect duty got fed up with her Form. Washed hair & had a bath. Bed: 10. 45 p.m.

Saturday 17th

My French form got accidently burnt & had to write a letter instead. Read quite a bit of Rebecca. Watched telly at night & tidied my bedroom. Bed: 1.5 a.m. (Had put clocks forward for last time.)

Sunday 18th

Read of lot of Rebecca & got fed up sitting. Had lamb for tea, it was nice. Took a photo of me & one of Topsy. At night funny film with Jerry Lewis in between discussing a holiday in Spain & I'm sure we won't go. Bed: 11.45 p.m.

Monday 19th

Read "Rebecca". Mum went early to go to town & Grandma's. Did project "Postcards & Places". Did washing up. In morning Mum sent note with David & Philip for Ian to make boiler up. Still in bed & they made a right row. Bed: 10.50 p.m.

Tuesday 20th
Had a very sore throat which started in the night. Made some cheese scones while Ian made some fudge. Finished "Rebecca" in bed in morning. Did washing up & that's all in afternoon. Was very foggy. Bed: 11.15 p.m.

Wednesday 21st
Had a rough night & was very ill in day. Stayed in bed & couldn't write my diary. It was last day of half term holiday.

Thursday 22nd
Had a very rough night. Seemed a little better in afternoon. Got a french pen friend called Christiane Martell. Ian went back to school. It hailed a little.

Friday 23rd
Was much better today & got up. Just read magazines in afternoon. Watched telly at night. Bed: 12.15 a.m.

Saturday 24th
Washed my hair & had a bath. Wrote letter to my French pen friend. Mum & Dad went out to Posh Club at night. Bed: 1 a.m.

Sunday 25th
Put my hair back into a kind of pony tail. It was cold but sun shined warm. Was going to church but mum was too tired. So taped "Darlin'" by Beach Boys. Had sore throat in morning. Bed: 10.30 p.m.

Monday 26th
Went back to school. Had to get my Tech. College leaflet. Heard about dance at Town Hall. Bed: 10.35 p.m.

Tuesday 27th *PANCAKE DAY.*
Still had my bad cold but played Hockey. Last 2 lessons in morning had lecture & film on the olympic games. Had to read "Jamaica Inn" for 2nd time in English. Bed: 10.45 p.m.

Wednesday 28th
Sun didn't shine all day & it was cold. Had science with a student. Nothing much happened. Bed: 11.5 p.m.

Thursday 29th
It is leap year & today is the extra day. Another cold day. Anne T. was away with flu. Bought dance tickets off Linda. Bed: 10.45 p.m.

March

Friday 1st

Ann F. went to her Grandad's funeral. It was a very cold day. Brenda was runner for interviews in afternoon. Played netball for first time since Christmas. Got our reports. Washed hair & had a bath. Bed: 11.20 p.m.

Saturday 2nd

Was miserable in morning 'cos fed up. Mum got her English course prospectus. In afternoon Dad took Ian to have haircut. Watched telly at night & Mr. Crowson came. Liz & Dave got married. Bed: 11.50 p.m.

Sunday 3rd

It was a bright sunny day but a bit chilly. Dad & Ian went to fly Ian's airplane with Topsy. Mum, Dad & Ian did a bit of gardening. Had a salad tea. Went to church. Bed: 10.55 p.m.

Monday 4th

It was quite a warm day. Was back late from dinner 'cos Anne was writing a note for Susan. Oral C.S.E. exam in Rm 11 (English) all day. Read some more of "Jamaica Inn" at night. Bed: 10.20 p.m.

Tuesday 5th

Got a bit windy by afternoon. Miss Malster had to go home with German measles. Had a letter from my French pen friend Christiane. Bed: 10.55 p.m.

Wednesday 6th

Was a very very windy day. Anne T. came back to school. In the evening it snowed quite a bit. Bed: 11.00 p.m.

Thursday 7th

Another very windy day with fine rain. Miss Newborn the headmistress came in, in cookery when we were all messing about. Nothing much happened. Bed: 10.35 p.m.

Friday 8th

The wind had died down. Heard about a nice comment from Vicky. Got our school photos, mine was terrible. Mum got her lesson from the ICS correspondence course. The first one with a lot to read. Just had a bath. Bed: 11.40 p.m.

Saturday 9th

Washed my hair & put it up 'cos couldn't do a thing with it. Dad & Ian went to town & got me a "Vanity Fair" magazine & I sent for a smashing offer of make-up. Watched film & "Invaders" at night. Dad went bowling. Bed: 12.25 a.m.

Sunday 10th

Was miserable 'because of headache & fed up. Finished "Jamaica Inn". Watched film "Her sister's Secret" for 2nd time. Went out to take Topsy for a walk around the new estate & on to the football ground. Played game of chess at night & I won.

Monday 11th

Did a lot of writing at school. Heard about a policeman coming round to bikes. Brenda was a little late to school. Lesley P. [Pycroft] had puncture & I walked a little way home with her.

Tuesday 12th

It was the warmest day since last summer. We had hockey & I was sweltering. Got new book to read in English "Tale of Two Cities". Saw Cilla Black show with Cliff Richards singing the Song for Europe called "Congratulations". Heard that I might not be able to go to the dance. Bed: 10.50 p.m.

Wednesday 13th

Can go to dance now (I think!). Miss Tatlow told us about Singapore. Nothing much happened. Bed: 10.45 p.m.

Thursday 14th

Came home in afternoon 'cos of bad stomach ache. Got a letter from French penfriend & wrote one back. It took me about 2 hours. Couldn't write my diary 'cos went straight to bed without having a wash or anything 'cos of stomach ache bad!

Friday 15th

Didn't have all that nice day at school. Met Mum from Perkins to go to town & get some shoes. Didn't see any I like & we were rushed. Came home. Washed hair & had a bath. Near 4 o'clock it rained hard & thundered. Bed 11.15 p.m.

Saturday 16th

Mum had bad migraine head but we still went up town & got me some new shoes & a new bag. I got a bad head but it finally went off. I went to dance at Dogsthorpe. It was smashing. Got sore feet. Bed 12.20 a.m.

Sunday 17th

Mum was in bed most of day with a migraine. Got up quite early. Pottered about the house doing jobs & didn't get fed up. Watched film, then took the dog for a walk & I was freezing. Came back & then Mr. & Mrs. Crowson, Anna & Claire came. Bed: 10.45 p.m.

Monday 18th

Talked about dance at school. Very windy day & had to go to school by myself in strong head wind, but lovely going home. Had Commonwealth visitors in school so got let out early at dinner time. Bed: 10.35 p.m.

Tuesday 19th

Another very windy day but not so much in the morning. Had hockey in the wind. It was budget day. Bed: 10.40 p.m.

Wednesday 20th

Another very windy day. Mr. Crowson came at night to measure up for the cupboards. Saw the episode of the "Virginian". Bed: 10.55 p.m.

Thursday 21st

The wind had died down because of the rain. Got soaked after dinner & when going home at ½ past 3. Got let out early because of prize giving. Had our last Maths lesson with Miss Baxter. Made soup in cookery in Rm. 3 'cos of refreshments made in Rm 2 for prizegiving. Bed: 10.40 p.m. Official 1st day of Spring.

Friday 22nd

Was quite a sunny day. Miss Malster was back & we had film slides of Switzerland in Geography. Washed hair & had bath. Got windy and rained at night. Bed: 11.35 p.m.

Saturday 23rd

Wrote nearly all day. Dad & Ian went to town but Dad felt ill with a rotten cold. At 7 o'clock that night I heard that I was going to the dance at the Tec. with Mum 'cos Dad felt rotten. Enjoyed myself.

Sunday 24th

Dad still felt rotten. Did not get fed up today. It rained quite a bit. Grandpa came in the afternoon. Played chess. Bed: 10.30 p.m.

Monday 25th

Was windy and there were many showers. Read some horrible tragedy poems in English. Dad spent most of the day in bed with his bad cold. Bed: 10.35 p.m.

Tuesday 26th

Was quite a warm day. Had hockey & got told off in it. Found out I could go swimming. Most teachers were stock taking. Bed: 10.25 p.m.

Wednesday 27th

Went to Town Hall with the school in the morning to see Council Chambers. Was quite a warm day. Bed: 11.5 p.m.

Thursday 28th

Was a very hot day. In cookery did some convenience foods & tasted them. Bed: 10.35 p.m.

Friday 29th

Another very hot day. Got my pink skirt finished. Had films on Switzerland in Geography. Had outdoor rounders. Did not wash my hair but had a bath. Mr. & Mrs. Crowson, Anna & Claire came. Mr. Crowson did the window pelmets. Bed: 11.20 p.m.

Saturday 30th

Was a much colder day. Mum went to a wedding. There were loads of weddings today because of tax rebate. Washed my hair Was Grand National day & Cambridge Oxford boat race. Mr. & Mrs. Bedford & Vicki came at night. Bed: 12.10 a.m.

Sunday 31st

Was a sunny day. Finished taking my photos. Dad came home to dinner from work. At night Mr. Crowson came to measure up for cupboards. Saw Gala Performance on telly. Bed: 10.35 p.m.

April

Monday 1st

Went to Tech. college for an hour to see grotty film & exhibition on Civil Engineering. Was a windy day. Gran & Grandpa came at night, there was a mix-up with Aunt Violet. Bed: 10.10 p.m.

Tuesday 2nd

It snowed nearly all day, a shock to everybody. It was Anne T.'s [Taylor] birthday. Brenda went to "Learning To Earning" by surprise. Miss Newborn told us about Tech. College exam. Will never have hockey again. Didn't have it for last time today 'cos of the snow. Bed: 10.35 p.m.

Wednesday 3rd

It was very cold. There were a few more snow showers but it had all melted by night. Brenda was late 'cos of puncture. Had film about spots in Science. Brenda & I talked about Scotland in English speech. Thundered twice. Virginian was good. Bed: 10.35 p.m.

Thursday 4th

Miss Ayres got married. Did some hard work cleaning the cookery room. Was very thirsty all day. Bed: 10.20 p.m.

Friday 5th

Was cold. Didn't do anything in needlework. In the afternoon we played a good game in Geog. Then came the time when the Easter leavers cried & a lot of others too. I didn't. Had a bath & Mum bought me some "Clearasil" for my face. Bed: 10.55 p.m.

Saturday 6th

Washed my hair. Played ball in garden. Rang Brenda & she said she was coming over. Saw Eurovision song contest at night. Spain won by one point above us. Dad went to a meeting & bowling. Bed: 11.55 p.m.

Sunday 7th

Didn't do much in day. At night Mr. Crowson, Anna & Claire came. Then Brenda's Dad, Maura & Annette came. Not long after Liz & Dave came & showed us photos of wedding. Bed: 12.15 a.m.

Monday 8th

We were all at home and in the garden. We let the bunny have a run. Had a bit of a cold. Cleaned out my bedroom and put Brenda's bed down. Bed: 10.20 p.m.

Tuesday 9th

Brenda came to stop in morning. Took Topsy out & then Meg. Had a go on Brenda's bike. Took Paul out & then Mark. Mark cried a lot. Bed: 11.25 p.m.

Wednesday 10th

We went to town, it was good fun. I had terrible stomach ache all afternoon. Watched telly at night. Bed: 11.30 p.m.

Thursday 11th

Took Topsy to playing fields & had a good time jumping dykes. Mum was at work full time. We took Mark out & then Brenda had to go home. Bed: 11.45 p.m.

Friday 12th *GOOD FRIDAY*
Mr. Crowson came in morning & afternoon to do cupboards. Read a lot of my library book "The Youngest Miss Mowbray". At night had a bit of a headache but washed my hair & had a bath. Bed: 10.55 p.m.

Saturday 13th
Went to town & got a groovy new dress. Got 2 Easter cards. One from Ruth & Roy & one from Sue in Wigan. Dad & Ian went to see "The Jungle Book" at the pictures. Afterwards they did some tyre kicking, which really means going to look at cars for sale Mr. Crowson came in the afternoon & did some more to the cupboards. Bed: 12.00 a.m.

Sunday 14th *EASTER SUNDAY*
Mr. Crowson came early in morning to do cupboards. Finished reading "The Youngest Miss Mowbray". Heard about the Dog nappers. Grandpa came in the afternoon. Mum & I went to church at night. Bed: 11.45 p.m.

Monday 15th *EASTER MONDAY*
Was a warm day. Took Mark out. Mr. Crowson came in morning. Heard that Daily Mirror were on strike. Grandma & Grandpa came in the evening. Bed: 11.35 p.m.

Tuesday 16th ✝
Mum was at work full time Had to collect Grandma's pension from the Post Office. Heard that little Karen had died [next door neighbour Karen Schuller aged 9 of leukemia]. *Rained all afternoon & I had a bad headache all day. Bed: 12.00 a.m.*

At the back Sally McDonald (me). Left to right Karen Schuller, Sally Lloyd, Ian McDonald, Ann Foster. Front row Lindsey Schuller. In the back garden of our bungalow 19 The Crescent, Eye, in about 1962.

Wednesday 17th

Mum still at work full time. My headache had gone off but was still there. Went to the bank for mum. Wrote 3 letters to my pen friends. Mr. Crowson came at night to frame Mum's paintings. Mrs. Una Hudson came round about a wreath. Bed: 11.35 p.m.

Thursday 18th

Went to Brenda's all day. (14 Everdon Way, Westwood Estate). *It was smashing. Walked a lot with Debbie, Annette and Andrew. Was quite a hot day but rained at night & early morning & thundered a bit. Bed: 11.15 p.m.*

Friday 19th

Still had my headache. Mum was still at work full time. Did a bit of my project. Had a bath. Bed: 11.20 p.m.

Saturday 20th

Had a lump behind my ear & phoned mum to come home. Karen's funeral. Had my hair done at the hair-dressers with Brenda. Looked awful. Went back to Brenda's & Brenda's Dad took us to the dance. Bed: 12.15 a.m.

Sunday 21st

Mum did the washing & I helped with the ironing. Grandpa came in afternoon. It was a hot day. Took Topsy for a walk round the new estate. Mr. & Mrs. Bedford & Vicki came at night. Still had the lump. Bed: 12.25 a.m.

Monday 22nd

Got the German Measles. Ian & Dad went to barbers & did some tyre kicking. Mum was still at work full time. Did the washing up then took Topsy for a walk. Dad & Ian came home with a car in mind. Mum came home & confirmed my German Measles. Bed: 10.30 p.m.

Tuesday 23rd

Was covered all over in spots except for my legs. Ian went back to school. Mum phoned about my Tech. College [entrance test] *to Miss Newborn. Was bored at home & did washing up. Saw good film at night it was a comedy called "Friends & Neighbours" with Arthur Askey. Bed: 10.55 p.m.*

Wednesday 24th

Got it worse on my arms especially at night when I thought it must have been the sun & wind. Did a lot of housework. Got quite a lot of spots on my face. Mrs. Hudson came round at night. Ann F. came & brought letter from Brenda. Bed: 10.20 p.m.

Thursday 25th

Should have done my Tech. College Exam today. Had more swollen glands, but the spots went down. Was quite a hot day. Did washing up & Mum's exam questions. Mum had been talking to Auntie Audrey & a lot of my school friends at work. Got hold of a new 5 penny & 10 penny piece. Bed: 10.25 p.m.

Friday 26th

Couldn't have bath or wash my hair. Mum forgot her coffee, she went to town. Got a letter from French pen pal & a picture from Beatles Fan club. Mum was tired out at night after being at work full time. Bed: 12.10 p.m.

Saturday 27th

Dave came in morning & Dad & him went "tyre kicking". Mum went with them & came back with fish 'n chips for dinner. Then Dad & Dave went again. Mr. Crowson, Anna & Claire came then. When Dad came back he had brought a white Triumph Herald car to show us & we went for a ride. Later he bought it. Gran & Grandpa came at night for a minute. Bed: 12.10 a.m.

Sunday 28th

(my other pen ran out). Had a bad headache. Was cloudy most of day. Gran & Grandpa came in afternoon. Before that, Dad, Ian & Topsy went to football field to fly plane. At night Mr. & Mrs. Bedford & Vicki came & I had to stay in my bedroom in case Vicki caught German measles. Bed:10.55 p.m.

Monday 29th

Mum was back to part time. Was a rainy day. Mum went to the Bank but they wouldn't lend her loan for car 'cos of 'credit squeeze'. Dad went to Shaw's for insurance. Did a bit of housework & that's all. Bed: 11.10 p.m.

Tuesday 30th

Rained all afternoon and didn't get my letter to Brenda 'cos Mum forgot to watch for Ann F. going to school. Didn't do much. Dad got fixed up with loan from U.D.T. Bed: 11.10 p.m.

Wednesday 1st
Rained all morning. Did quite a lot of housework. Brenda sent me a letter which Mrs. Burt had read. Mr. Crowson came & did front door handles. Dad brought car home & put it in garage. Bed: 11.00 p m.

Thursday 2nd
Rained a lot again. Did washing up & read half of "Village School" book from school. Felt depressed at night. Washed out the ashtrays of car in morning with Topsy. Bed 11.10 p.m.

Friday 3rd
It was fine but cold. Washed my hair & had a bath. At night we went to Aunty Lucy's in the car. Weighed myself on Aunty Joyce's bathroom scales & I was down from 9 st to 8½ stone. I was very pleased. Bed: 11.40 p.m.

Saturday 4th
Baked a cake & tidied kitchen. Mum & Ian were busy on the garden. At night went to the phone box and rang Brenda. Then we went to Mr. & Mrs. Bedford's & it rained. Bed: 11.30 p.m.

Sunday 5th
Did a lot of work, but Mum did loads, the garden & the house. Mr. & Mrs. Crowson, Anna & Claire came. At night, Mr. & Mrs. Sismore & Michael came. Bed: 10.50 p.m.

Monday 6th
It was my first day back to school for a month. Went swimming in morning. Rained going home from school. Bed: 10.25

Tuesday 7th
Rained a lot. Nothing much happened but had quite a bit of homework like yesterday. Bed: 11.10 p.m.

Wednesday 8th *C.* [Christopher Goodall's birthday, Nottingham]
Brenda was out in the morning at Cavisteed nursery. Rained heavily coming back from dinner & got soaked. In afternoon went to see "Swan Lake" at the Embassy. Had a good time but got home late at 7.30 p.m. Bed: 10.15 p.m.

Thursday 9th
Did not write my diary 'cos went to bed straight away with stomach ache. Had the day off school because of voting. Bed: 9.30 p.m.

Friday 10th

Another rainy day. Benda came home with me at night to stay at her Nannie's for 3 weeks. Washed hair & had a bath. Bed: 11.40 p.m.

Saturday 11th

Went to town in car with Brenda. Got some things on Wines in France for my project & covered my R.E. project in afternoon. A bit mild & rainy. Dad went bowling & Brenda came a little while at night & Mr. Crowson for his money. Got ready for going to Hunstanton in morning. Bed: 11.00 p.m.

Sunday 12th

Mum wasn't very well, she had a Migraine attack so Dad, Ian, Topsy & I went to Hunstanton. Wind was cold but walked a lot. Had a good day. Bed: 10.15 p.m.

Monday 13th

Rained hard in the morning. Went to school with Brenda & Ann F. Never went swimming. Had disagreement over date of Whitsun. Brenda came at night & we took the dog for a walk. Bed: 10.45 p.m.

Tuesday 14th

Ann F. went in the car. Sharing classrooms all morning 'cos of C.S.E. exams. Had my first tennis & rounders since last year. Talking about Christian Aid week (this week) in history. Brenda came for a little while at night.

Wednesday 15th

A windy but warm day. Did gardening in science. Ann T. & I heard when our Tech. exam was gonna be. Brenda came at night. Did a bit of homework and went for a walk. Bed: 11.15 p.m.

Thursday 16th

Made chocolate eclairs in Cookery. Miss Newborn saw us at break about our Tech. exam. In Art we saw C.S.E. work. Brenda didn't bike home with me 'cos she went swimming practise for life saving. She came for an hour at night. Bed: 10.50 p.m.

Friday 17th

It was Ann Harrison's and Ann Foster's birthday. Did theory in needlework. Had argument with Brenda in afternoon & sent her to Coventry. We were talking in tennis. Brenda went to stay at Linda's. Washed hair & had a bath. Mum & Dad had gone to town then on to Jill & John's. Bed: 11.55 p.m.

Saturday 18th

Didn't get up too early. Brenda came with rotten cold. Washed her hair & tried to curl it, but didn't work out. I baked a cake. We did a bit of Geography homework. Brenda went with my money for ticket for dance. At night we went to see Mr. & Mrs. Cranswick, Sandra & Elizabeth (friend). Bed 11.25 p.m.

Sunday 19th

Iced my cake, cleaned up & did my homework. First Grandpa came, then the Greens and then the Kendles. Saw Bedfords come but turn away! Bed: 11.10 p.m.

Monday 20th

Went to do my Tech. exam & had a good time. Had to go back to school but I was the only one. Was a very cold day. Heard of girls that had passed. Brenda came round & she did her needlework - her dress for the dance. Mum went to Chinese Restaurant at night. Bed: 10.55 p.m.

Tuesday 21st

Got sorted out about the dance & about my reading in prayers. Anne T. was off with a cold. Brenda went for interview at Tech & found she'd passed. [childcare course] *Had a lot of homework. Bed: 11.5 p.m.*

Wednesday 22nd

Has been very cold. Had to practise my reading in History. Heard that Anne T. had passed her G.C.E. course Tech exam. Had to think about Open Evening in Science. Bed: 10.45 p.m.

Thursday 23rd

Got sorted out in cookery about our dinner & heard about some stupid assignments we had got to do. Anne T. came back after dinner. Was a much warmer day. Brenda saw the Hollies at her Mum's cafe. Bed: 10.15 p.m.

Friday 24th

Was another warm day. Anne T. was off again. Had film on diseases in Geog. Brenda came home with me & we washed my hair & nearly finished her dress. While we were in bedroom, Mr. & Mrs. Crowson, Anna & Claire came. Bed: 11.55 p.m.

Saturday 25th

Dad, Ian & I went to town. It was raining, but went to Dad's friend's house first. At night went to dance & it was still raining. Bed: 12.10 a.m. P.S. Hair looked terrible.

Sunday 26th

Dad had to go to work 'cos someone was off. Quite a warm day. Did my homework & projects. At night we went between Eye & Newborough teaching Mum to drive. Bed: 10.37 p.m.

Monday 27th

Went swimming in morning. Was quite a hot day. Talked about the dance & Lynda P. Saw round Brenda's Nannie's bungalow. Had a lot of homework (as usual). Bed: 11.7 p.m.

Tuesday 28th

Was misty in morning but very hot in afternoon. We had our cycling proficiency and badges were handed out in the hall. Then we were let out earlier. Saw Margaret Gray outside. Bed:10.45 p.m. P.S. Got my letter to say I'd passed Tech. exam.

Wednesday 29th

Did my reading on stage in Assembly and I shook something terrible and mumbled quietly instead of reading out loud. Was foggy to start with but a really hot day. Got a puncture. Bed: 11.10 p.m.

Thursday 30th

Had to do my dinner in cooking it was terrible eating it.[a meal for the teachers and to eat it with them] *Had a puncture & had to walk home by myself. Hot in afternoon & did sketch of school in art. Bed: 11.00 p.m.*

Friday 31st

Was a very hot day. Brenda & I had a picnic & sunbathed for an hour. Got parcel from Phyllis. Washed hair & had a bath. Bed: 11.35 p.m.

June

Saturday 1st

Brenda & I went for walk with Topsy in morning. We sunbathed all afternoon & got rather sunburnt. It was a very hot day. At night Dad & I went to see Grandma & Grandpa & then went on to Auntie Sheila's but they weren't there. Came home & made up some sandwiches. Bed: 10.45 p.m.

Sunday 2nd *WHITSUN*

Went to Matlock in Derbyshire. Lovely hills & countryside but got a bit jarred with travelling. Did 194 miles altogether. Went through Nottingham. Was a hot day. Mum was a bit ill with travelling. Bed: 11.15 p.m.

Monday 3rd *WHIT MONDAY*
*Sat in sun nearly all day & got a tan on my face but spots on my arms & legs.
Mr. Crowson came in morning, but Dad was at work. At night Grandpa &
Grandma came & Dad went to bowling match. Bed: 12.30 a.m.*

Tuesday 4th
*Was a dull day & rained. Did my homework & French project. Was a colder
day & had bad headache. Saw repeat of good film called "The Smallest
show on Earth" it was funny. Bed: 12.5 a.m.*

Wednesday 5th
*Was another dull day. Heard that Robert Kennedy had been shot. Rang
Brenda up about tomorrow but she wasn't there. Ann F. had friend Marilyn
over. Did a lot of my French project & some of my R.E. Bed: 11.20 p.m.*

Thursday 6th
*Went to Brenda's. Did a bit of tennis with Brenda in morning, then took
Annette & Andrew round Netherton Estate. Came home on an earlier bus.
Had rotten headache at night. Robert Kennedy died. Bed: 11.55 p.m.*

Friday 7th
*Felt lazy. Washed hair & had a bath. Had to make Ian pancakes for dinner.
Kept clouding over. Watched telly at night. Hair came out nicer. Bed: 11.20
p.m.*

Saturday 8th *Did not do much in the day. Kept clouding over again. At night
Mr. & Mrs. Cranswick & Sandra came. They left Sandra with me while they
went to the Bull in Westgate. Before that we had our photos taken in the
back garden (Sandra & I) by Mr. Cranswick. Bed: 12.30 a.m.*

Sunday 9th ✝
Was a sunny hot day. The bunny died at 2 p.m. Sunbathed and took up the hem of my school dress & wrote a letter to my penfriend (Swedish). Mr. Crowson came & wanted us to go to tea (we didn't). Mum & I went to church at night. Bed: 10.55 p.m.

Monday 10th
Didn't go swimming 'cos didn't fancy it. Was a hot day. Brenda is spending the week down at Wells. Had my hair down for school. Bed: 10.40 p.m.

Tuesday 11th
Was a dull day. Did tennis all games lesson 'cos of others practising athletics. Nothing much happened. Bed: 10.45 p.m.

Wednesday 12th
Sat near Audrey Leonard nearly all day. Ann T. was in happy mood & going round with Vicky. Was asked to do Lyn Misen's prefect duty for next week Form 2A1. Went to see brass rubbings in Christchurch last two lessons. Bed: 11.20 p.m.

Thursday 13th
Was a windy day. Did assignment in cookery & Mrs. Hall got on my nerves. Had to eat what I cooked at Grandma's & gave her most of it. Got a postcard from Mr. & Mrs. Bedford & Vicki down at Folkestone. Bed: 11.5 p.m.

Friday 14th
Sat with Audrey in all the lessons & we talked about going to Salvation Army youth club. Washed hair & had a bath. Was a windy day. Bed: 11.55 p.m.

Saturday 15th
Cleaned out my bedroom & the bottom drawer of my dressing table. Phoned Audrey up, but she wasn't there. Phoned Brenda up in afternoon & she told me about her MARVELLOUS holiday. Watched telly at night. Bed: 11.50 p.m.

Sunday 16th
Was dull & rained in afternoon. Dad brought some strawberries home (first this year). The Bedfords came & talked about their holiday at Folkestone & gave us the address, (some hopes). Went to Milton Ferry & decided it was a long way to walk. Toured round Longthorpe Estate & came home. Bed: 10.45 p.m.

Monday 17th

Brenda came back & we had a good talk about her holidays. Mrs. Barber told me off about swapping prefects duty. Hair was nice to begin with but terrible & frizzy at night. Went with Audrey walking to Milton Ferry with Salvation Army Youth Club. Didn't like it much. Bed: 11.15 p.m. P.S. Eastern Ave. had been "re-chipped" & Dad phoned up about holidays.

Tuesday 18th

Helped Brenda out in prefect's duty. Got told off in Games for changing in toilets by Mrs. Handley. Did a lot of hunting for holiday photos at night to put in a scrap book. Bed: 11.15 p.m.

Wednesday 19th

Had the day off 'cos some girls & teachers were going to Parliament & some to the zoo. Got up quite late and did my homework, projects & washing-up. Had my hair up. Was a dull day. Bed: 11.00 p.m.

Thursday 20th

Finished my picture of drawing the school. Found that there were no vacancies at "Little Switzerland" for our holidays. Brenda's Dad said she could have pony "Velvet Princess". Thundered and lightened on way home on my bike, I was scared. Made cake at night for Garden Fete.

Friday 21st *THE LONGEST DAY*

Sky kept clouding over & a little of thunder & lightning. Grandma had won a £25 on the premium bonds (her 9th win). Saw Part 1 of "Wuthering Heights" on telly late at night. Washed hair & had a bath. Bed: 11.45 p.m.

Saturday 22nd

Rained nearly all day. Went to a new shop called "Ratio" in Fengate. Decided and prepared to go to London tomorrow. Bed: 10.20 p.m.

Sunday 23rd

We went to London & went round Petticoat Lane market, London Bridge & Heathrow airport. Had a gorgeous day but was tired & had a headache at night. Kept clouding over & raining, but didn't spoil our day. Bed: 10.20 p.m.

Monday 24th

Was a cold day. Went swimming with school. Rained in the day. Heard about visitors we missed yesterday. Did my projects at night. Rotten reception on telly. Bed: 10.30 p.m.

Tuesday 25th

Rained nearly all day. Police woman came to talk to us at school & our photo was taken. Made a sponge at night for open evening. Did my R.E. project. Told Mum I wanted to stay on with the rest if we weren't going on holiday. Bed: 11.00 p.m.

Wednesday 26th

Brenda went to Lawn Avenue Nursery in morning. Had lot of homework. Finished my Gladys Aylward, R.E. project. Decorated my cake. Bed: 11.5 p.m.

Thursday 27th

Helped all day with preparations for open evening. Made three Victoria Sandwiches in cookery & had blisters to prove it. Was very windy. Went to open evening & had a good time. Bed: 11.20 p.m.

Friday 28th

Rained nearly all day & lightened and thundered in evening. Did nothing all morning except watch shows (from last night) & walk round school. Did not do much in afternoon either. Washed hair & had bath. Bed: 11.50 p.m.

Saturday 29th

Did not get up till dinner time. Had letter from Tech. about the rules (hockey ugh!). [Wednesday afternoon sports] Grandma & Grandpa came. Brenda came over & did her hair then we went to a dance. Did not seem to like it till about 10 p.m. Bed: 12.15 a.m.

Sunday 30th

Was a very hot day. Said on wireless it was hottest day this year. Did not do much in day. Mum & Dad went to Sismore's at night. Bed: 11.10 p.m.

July

Monday 1st

It has been the hottest July 1st for 7 years. Was sweltering so did not do much in afternoon at school. Went swimming & it was fab. Didn't sleep well the night before 'cos hot. Bed: 10.35 p.m. P.S. Got some Sahara desert dust, only falls about every 15 years.

Tuesday 2nd

Was nearly as hot. In afternoon was our school sports. Sat on grass hill & watched. Had been violent floods & thunderstorms in some places. Bed: 11.00 p.m.

Wednesday 3rd
Was a cold wind. Got our R.E. results on our projects. Brenda rang up about jobs for us at Woolworths. Bed: 11.20 p.m.

Thursday 4th *AMERICAN INDEPENDENCE DAY.*
Saw Alec Rose sail home on telly at Gran's at dinner time. Saw Swedish girl over here to stay for a while. Rang Woolworths up, but forgot it was half day closing. (silly me!) Bed: 10.40 p.m.

Friday 5th
Had a cold. Brenda seemed to be in an awkward mood. Swedish girl Eva came to school. Rang up Woolworths dinner time & night. Didn't get a job. Found an ideal Sat. job in paper. Rang Brenda up twice 'cos wanted to go to this dance but Brenda couldn't. Quite a warm day. Bed: 12.5 a.m.

Saturday 6th
Went to town in morning for an interview for a job at Britannia Studios. Didn't seem very hopeful. Felt tired with my cold in afternoon. Bed: 10.40 p.m.

Sunday 7th
Went to Cromer. Weather wasn't too bad. I was jarred there, but we got our caravan booked. Mum had headache & so did I. Bed: 9.30 p.m.

Monday 8th
Rained quite a lot. Had to finish my English folder. Listened to Soul music in Music. Had junior school girls, who were coming to John Mansfield after the summer, looking around the school. Bed: 10.40 p.m.

Tuesday 9th
Mum went to work "all day" but had to come home at dinner time 'cos she felt ill with her migraine attack. Was a hot day. Had more junior school children round in afternoon. Nearly finished my French project by doing a lot at night. Got letter to confirm our caravan. Annette's pic. in Advertiser when she won baby contest. Bed: 11.00 p.m.

Wednesday 10th
Mum went to work full time. Rained all day very hard. Did a lot to my Needlework at night & finished my French folder. Had to show Miss Newborn my English folder 'cos it was "beautifully neat". Bed: 11.10 p.m.

Thursday 11th

It rained and stormed all night & in the morning. In the West it was reported to be worst floods for 20 years. Here, there were floods especially at Newark. Car Dyke was very much swollen. Couldn't go to school till after dinner & there was big lake on playing field. Missed the party in dinner hour. Was fine all afternoon & evening. Bed: 11.00 p.m.

Friday 12th

I left school today for good. Finished my blouse in needlework. Went to Town Hall in afternoon to Treasurer's Dept. was boring. Got back to school late I could not cry about leaving 'cos everyone was making jokes (they weren't leaving but staying on into 5th form to take CSE exams). Washed hair, had bath at night. Gran & Grandpa came. Watched Part 4, the last of Wuthering Heights. Bed: 11.45 p.m.

Saturday 13th

Went for job in morning. Didn't get one. Packed all afternoon. It was a mild day. At night Dad came home. Had tea & then started off about 7.30, arrived safely at about 8.30. Cleaned caravan out & looked at sea. Was cold at night.

Sunday 14th

Got up early and walked along cliffs to beach. There were a few showers but it was quite warm and sunny in the afternoon. We played tennis a lot. Then we took a walk up to Sheringham in the evening. Was a lovely sunset & lovely view from hill.

Monday 15th

Went to Cromer in morning & it poured of rain. Played tennis a bit but stayed in most of time 'cos it was cold. I was jarred.

Tuesday 16th

Was almost as bad as yesterday but did not rain as much. Played tennis in morning with 2 little boys. Wrote some postcards in late afternoon we went to Sheringham. It is nice there.

Wednesday 17th

Was very windy all night & all day. Got up late & went down to village. In evening went with Topsy up the hill to Sheringham. Was a very windy journey.

Thursday 18th

Was rotten wet weather in morning so read magazines in caravan. Weather brightened in afternoon so played tennis with 2 girls, Vivienne & Barbara. Was nice & sunny at night so we went for a walk along cliffs towards Cromer & took some photos.

Friday 19th

Was a glorious day. Ian & I went up the hill & took some photos & one on the beach. Played tennis quite a lot, then went down to beach & paddled. Got sunburnt red then went into Sheringham at night & got some fish & chips.

Saturday 20th

Mum got the caravan cleaned & we left at 11 a.m. We spent the rest of the day at Wells, on the beach & round the few shops & in the "Pop Inn". When we got home after stopping in Wisbech for food for tea, I phoned Brenda but she was not there. Bed: 12.15 a.m.

Sunday 21st *DAD'S BIRTHDAY, 40 years old.*

Washed my hair & had a bath. Grandma & Grandpa came. Had a long chat with Brenda on phone at night, then watched a Bob Hope "Road" film. Bed: 11.40 p.m.

Monday 22nd

Dad went to town in morning. Got up late. Got postcard from Audrey, touring Scotland. Rang Brenda at night & had a long chat. Wrote a long letter to my French pen friend at night. Bed: 12.5 a.m.

Tuesday 23rd

It rained a bit. We went to town in the dinner hour. Had to make "Casserole of Beef" for tea. The central heating man came down about our leaking tank. Rang Brenda up again & had a long chat. Bed: 12.5 a.m.

Wednesday 24th

Dad went to help a man with a car in morning. Derek the plumber came down to mend the tank. Phoned about 5 jobs. Jill & John, Angela & David came at night. Bed: 12.5 a.m.

Thursday 25th

In afternoon went to Castor Backwaters fishing (didn't catch anything!). Before tea, Dad, Ian & I went over quickly to Jill & John's. After tea Brenda came round. We went for a walk after "Top of the Pops". Bed: 12.5 a.m.

Friday 26th

Was a rotten day. We were going to go to Wicksteed Park but we didn't. Phoned up Co-op, but no luck. So Mum & I went to Arcade Agency & I filled in a form. On way back called to see Grandma & Grandpa. Washed hair & had a bath. Had late tea. Bed: 10.45 p.m.

Saturday 27th

Dad was watching cricket on the telly. Dad, Ian & I went to town. Dad took me to Brenda's at night to baby sit. Bed: 12.00 a.m.

Sunday 28th

Mum had a bad headache so she stayed at home while Dad, Ian, Topsy & I went to Wicksteed Park. Called round for Brenda but she was out riding. Just before we went home we met Mr. & Mrs. Healey & Shaun. Came back, had tea & watched a Bob Hope film. Bed: 11.30 p.m.

Monday 29th

Mum still had her migraine attack but she went to work. Dad was on nights so we took Mum to work then paid quick visits to Jill's, Grandma's and Mrs. Bedford's It was a coldish day. Bed: 11.35 p.m.

Tuesday 30th

Mum kept being sick & stayed in bed all morning yet went to work. I did housework most of the day while Ian watched cricket on the telly. Bed: 11.30 p.m.

Wednesday 31st

Was a dull day & rained a bit. Did a bit of housework & made a jam tart. Grandpa came at night. Mum was better. Bed: 11.35 p.m.

August

Thursday 1st

Looked out some silver paper & stamps for the "Peterborough Standard" & kept myself busy so as not to get bored. Ian & I took Topsy for a walk. At night I was taping songs & got jarred. Brenda's Dad popped in to say that Brenda couldn't come to pictures with me. Bed: 12.5 p.m.

Friday 2nd

Washed my hair & had a bath. It drizzled all day & the house was in a mess. Watched telly at night & stuck some stamps in my books. Topsy didn't seem very well in morning but was all right in afternoon. Phoned Brenda but she hadn't a lot to say. Bed: 12.30 a.m.
P.S. Had to get up about 1.30 a.m. to get a hot water bottle. I already had my dressing gown on & it was the MIDDLE OF SUMMER.

Saturday 3rd

Got up very late at dinner time. Went to town & I got a cheap dress in the sales. Mum drove the car home. After tea, Mr. & Mrs. Bedford & Vicki came but I went to babysit for Mr. & Mrs. Canham. Bed: 12.15 a.m.

Sunday 4th

Got up late again. Was bored until we went out for a driving lesson with Mum through the town. After tea we went to Grandma & Grandpa's. Bed: 12.00 a.m.

Monday 5th

Weather was a bit better. Helped Ian to cut the grass. Took Topsy for a walk. I.T.V. are still on strike. Made new picture design for my bedroom at night. Bed:

Tuesday 6th

Weather was miserable again. Had rheumatism in my shoulders all day. Didn't do much 'cos of this. Bed: 11.45 p.m.

Wednesday 7th

Weather wet & windy again. My shoulders were a bit better. I was bored & cold all day. Bed: 12.00 a.m.

Thursday 8th

Ian & I took the dog for a walk. We came back & did the washing up. then I made a cake for Grandpa's birthday. Rained a bit in the morning. Bed: 11.20 p.m.

Friday 9th

Had the stomach ache terribly & was sick on my carpet. Spent most of day in bed. Rained a lot all night & in the morning. A few floods again. Said on news that it was dullest August so far that has ever been recorded since records began in 1929. Went to Gran's at night to take Grandpa his birthday things. Bed: 11.10 p.m.

Saturday 10th

Washed my hair & had a bath. The sun shone for once. Made some tarts for tea. Dad went to a bowling match at night. There was a dance on at Eye. I phoned Brenda. Bed: 11.30 p.m.

Sunday 11th

A change in the weather, it was hot. Sunbathed a bit but was fed up. At night Mum & I went to church. Finished my "White Twilight" book. Bed: 11.45 p.m.

Monday 12th

Was another lovely hot day. We took Mum to work & then went to town & Grandma's & Ian had his hair cut. Met Jill, John, Angela & David in town. At night Mr. & Mrs. Hasty & Colin came. Bed: 11.40 p.m.

Tuesday 13th

It rained quite a bit. Did some dusting then wrote all afternoon. Nothing much happened. Bed: 11.15 p.m.

Wednesday 14th

Rained on & off but mostly on. Took dog for a long walk. Did a bit of housework & then wrote a letter to my french pen friend. At night I went out and rang Brenda for a long chat. Bed: 11.30 p.m.

Thursday 15th

Was lovely sunny morning. Took Topsy for a walk. Did washing up & looked through my library books. Rained nearly all afternoon. Changed my bedroom round a bit at night. Bed: 11.45 p.m.

Friday 16th

Washed my hair & had a bath. Was a nice day in the morning but rained in afternoon. I.T.V. strike ended. My hair looked nice. Bed: 12.15 a.m.

Saturday 17th

We went to town. At night I went to pictures with Brenda. Bed: 11.45 p.m.

Sunday 18th

Was a sunny day but a bit windy. Was getting the dinner prepared when I cut my thumb. Posted Angela's birthday card. Grandpa came in afternoon. Bed: 11.5 p.m.

Monday 19th

Got up early to go to Angela's & Jill's in morning but my bike had a puncture. Rained a little in the afternoon & was windy & cold. Read a lot of my book "The Sisters' Tale". Thundered a bit at night. Bed: 11.25 p.m.

Tuesday 20th

Our Jones cousins Andrew, Simon & all from Newport came in morning but Ian & I were in bed & Mum had gone for her driving lesson. Walked to Grandma's in afternoon & stayed there. When we got home Simon & Andrew & all were there again. They came later after tea. Bed: 12.15 a.m.

Wednesday 21st
Mum went into work full-time. Ian & I went to the Fletchers & then to the bowling alley & then back again. Uncle Billy finally took us home. Was a hot day. Bed: 10.30 p.m.

Thursday 22nd
It was a very hot day & Mum was still at work full time. Most of the day I sat on the bed eating ice cubes. I cut the grass in stages. Bed: 11.25 p.m.

Friday 23rd
Was foggy in the morning & I got up early. Washed my hair & had a bath. Was another very hot day. Bed: 12.15 a.m.

Saturday 24th
Mum went to work in the morning. Didn't do much in the day. Went to Brenda's at night & we went down the Halcyon but we were bored. Bed: 12.30 a.m.

Sunday 25th
Did a bit of housework & the dinner. We were going to to to church but didn't. Put my hair up, it was a windy day. Did some taping, took Topsy for a walk. Mr. & Mrs. Bedford & Vicki came at night. Bed: 12.25 a.m.

Monday 26th
Mum was at work full time. Dad, Ian & I went to Grandma's & then to town. Was a windy but warm day. Bed: 11 p.m.

Tuesday 27th
Was a windy day again. Did a bit of housework & then went to hairdressers & had my hair trimmed. Didn't do much for the rest of the day. Bed: 11.15 p.m.

Wednesday 28th
Got a bit jarred in the day. Did a bit of housework & we took Topsy for a walk. Got my booklet "Land of the Living Dragon". Cooked the tea at night & then rang Brenda. Rained in the evening. Bed: 11.10 p.m.

Thursday 29th *Ian's Birthday.*
We got a lot of letters besides Ian's cards. Rained a lot & was a damp, cold,

dull old day. After taking Topsy for a walk, doing a bit of housework & learning Chinese, I cooked the tea again. Grandpa came at night. Bed: 11.25 p.m.

Friday 30th
Washed my hair & had a bath. Made the tea. At night went to Perkins club dance with Brenda, it was o.k. Came home late, but still watched my Chinese programme. Bed: 12.30 a.m.

Saturday 31st
Mum spent all day in bed. Dad, Ian & I went to town & it poured of rain. The rest of the time I was real bored, but did a bit of housework. Bed: 11.45 p.m.

September

Sunday 1st
In the morning Auntie Hanny & Grandad McDonald came on their way home from Switzerland. Spent most of the day talking & at night looked at their films. Rained nearly all day with only a few bright bits. Bed: 11.55 p.m.

Monday 2nd
After waiting for the car to be repaired, Auntie Hanny & Grandad went about dinner time & we took them as far as the A.1. At night mum & I went to see "Son et Lumiere" at the Cathedral. Bed: 11.45 p.m.

Tuesday 3rd
Went up town & got some gorgeous health sandals. Called on Grandma's. It was quite a hot day. Bed: 11.45 p.m.

Wednesday 4th
Got a telegram to say that Uncle Kenneth was coming at 3.15 on the train. Dad & Ian went fishing with Dave & caught a fish to keep but mum said to take it back so they did. Washed my hair & had a bath. Bed: 10.5 p.m.

Thursday 5th
Ian started back to school. At 3.30 A.M. Dad & I got up & met Uncle Kenneth off the train, I enjoyed going to the station in the middle of the night. After breakfast Dad, Kenneth & I went & cut Grandma's lawn, then took me to collect my report from school. I cut our back grass when we got home for the exercise. At night Mr. Houldershaw came with party tickets. Bed: 11.45 p.m.

Friday 6th

In the afternoon, Dad, Ken & I went to Mrs. Cranswicks & then to town. At night we went to Longthorpe sausage & cider party, while Dad, Ian & Ken went with Brenda's Dad to the pistol club. Bed: 12.30 a.m.

Saturday 7th

Felt depressed in the morning. Then Dad, Ken, Ian & I went to town. Was a hot day in the sun. Ian & Ken spent all evening making up model aeroplanes. At midnight Dad, Ian & I took Ken up to the station. Bed: 12.40 a.m.

Sunday 8th

Got up late & Grandpa came. Was quite a hot day, so after making the dinner I sunbathed a bit. In the evening Mr. & Mrs. Hasty came. They went & we watched the first episode of "The Forsyte Saga". Bed: 10.55 p.m.

Monday 9th

I was on my own all day, so Topsy & I walked up to Grandma's & took the pension. [5.6 mile round trip] I cut the grass then Grandma's friends came. It was a hot day. Bed: 11.50 p.m.

Tuesday 10th

Was another hot day. Mum was only working part time. After doing a bit of housework & going up the shop I took Martin for an hour's walk in his pram. Jill, John, Angela & David came at night. Bed: 11.20 p.m.

Wednesday 11th

Got up late & Mum was at work full time, so I was all on my own. Did quite a bit of housework & then sat down to do a competition. It rained all day. After waiting a long time in the rain to speak to Brenda only had a very short talk. Bed: 11.15 p.m.

Thursday 12th

Got up a bit earlier, Mum was full time again so I was on my own. Took Topsy for a long walk on the football field & picked a few blackberries. Didn't do much else. Bed: 11.40 p.m.

Friday 13th

It was Friday the 13th. Had a bath, washed & set my hair in an hour. Mum went for a driving lesson & when she came back I was still in bed. Was a fine day. Bed: 12.15 a.m.

Saturday 14th

Got up late. Spent all afternoon at Perkins open day. Rained a lot. Legs ached at night. Went to babysit for the Canhams. Bed: 11.30 p.m.

Sunday 15th
Got up earlier. Prepared the dinner. Grandpa came. Mum restarted the central heating as it was wet windy & cold. There were many floods in other places. Spent the afternoon at an "All Stars" charity football match with Ann Peacock & her friend. It was good but I got wet and windswept. Mum works with Ann from the Tech. Bed: 11.10 p.m.

Monday 16th
Was raining hard & very windy. Heard of bad floods in the South-East. Went to town & Grandma's with Dad in afternoon. Rained all the time. Dad still had a bad stomach. Bed: 12.10 a.m.

Tuesday 17th
Rained a bit in the morning, but was dry all afternoon. Got up late & Mum went for a driving lesson. Took baby Martin out in the afternoon. Did a bit of housework & cut the back grass at night. Bed: 11.10 p.m.

Wednesday 18th
Was a fine day again. Got up earlier. In the afternoon Topsy & I walked up to Grandma's & I cut the grass. Bed: 11.20 p.m.

Thursday 19th
Was a fine day with a cold wind. Took Topsy diking! Didn't do anything special. Bed: 11.30 p.m.

Friday 20th
It was a windy dull rainy thundery day. Washed my hair & had a bath. Bed: 12.15 a.m.

Saturday 21st
Dad dropped me off to do some shopping while he fetched some posts. Was a very windy day. Came back on bus & did a bit of housework as mum was doing washing. Dad went out bowling at night & the telly went wrong. Bed: 11.10 p.m.

Sunday 22nd
Got up quite early & we went to Nottingham. Had a satisfying day, but got home a bit late. Bed: 11.00 p.m. [Probably to see Roy, Ruth & Andrew Eggleshaw and Christopher Goodall, friends of parents]

Monday 23rd
Started at the Technical College today. It was a bit hectic & muddling. The weather was bad. It rained & lightened and thundered. The telly had been taken away to be mended for the evening. Bed: 10.35 p.m.

Tuesday 24th
Was a better day at the Tech College. At night Dad took us to a second hand shop to get a telly. Bed: 10.40 p.m.

Wednesday 25th
Was foggy in the morning. The day was okay. Our old telly was brought back. Bed: 10.50 p.m.

Thursday 26th
Got wet in morning. Typing was hard again. Didn't have Games 'cos it was a bit wet. Bed: 10.55 p.m.

Friday 27th
Last day of week. My hair felt a mess. At night we went to the Piccavers only. Brenda wasn't there. Washed my hair & had a bath rather late at night. Bed: 12.45 a.m.

Saturday 28th
Was a windy day. Went to town by myself. Got a yellow blouse that had to be altered. Mum & Dad went to Posh Club at night. Bed: 12.15 a.m.

Sunday 29th
Felt rotten with my cold all day. Grandpa came in early afternoon. Bill from Cambridge came at night. Bed: 10.20 a.m.

Monday 30th
Got a headache at Tech with all the concentration in typing. Was quite a cold day. Bed: 10.30 p.m.

October

Tuesday 1st
Met a girl at Tech. who lives next door to Auntie Audrey. Rained all afternoon. Had dinner with Brenda & Helen 'cos Barbara wasn't there. Had films in General Studies. Bed: 10.30 p.m.

Wednesday 2nd
Had a demonstration with two electric typewriters last lesson. Had a bit of homework to do at night. Bed: 10.50 p.m.

Thursday 3rd
Had a not very nice day at Tech. and even hockey wasn't too bad. Had quite a lot of homework. Brenda was away. Stayed fine and quite mild all day. Bed: 10.45 p.m.

Friday 4th

Went to Wirrina Youth Stadium in last lesson for something to do with expansion. Wasn't a bad day. Got a lift home with Julia's mum at night. Washed my hair & had a bath but was very tired so went to bed early.

Saturday 5th

Went to town with Dad & Ian. Got some new black shoes. Went round to Piccavers & picked up some potatoes. Cleaned my bedroom, did my homework, & watched a good film with Glynis Johns in, at night. Bed: 12.15 a.m.

Sunday 6th

We all did a few gardening jobs in the morning. In the afternoon went to Bill's in Cambridge. Walked round colleges, had tea, watched telly & played with kitten. Had a good day & the weather was good. Bed: 10.55 p.m.

Monday 7th

Wasn't too bad a day at Tech. Was a nice sunny day. Bed: 10.45 p.m.

Tuesday 8th

Didn't have a very good day at Tech. Rained all day. Finished "How Green Was my Valley". It was sad. Bed: 10.55 p.m.

Wednesday 9th

Was a better day at Tech. Kept fine all day. Bed: 10.25 p.m.

Thursday 10th

Wasn't too bad a day. Had dinner with Jean & friends instead of Barbara. Had to play rounders in games. Bed: 10.25 p.m.

Friday 11th

Quite a good day. Mum bought a gorgeous new evening dress. Washed hair & had a bath at night. Mum & Dad went to dancing lessons. Bed: 11.15 p.m.

Saturday 12th

Went to town & met Margaret Gray. It was a windy day. At night went to a dance at Dogsthorpe. It was very good & Brenda enjoyed it too!! Bed: 12.15 a.m.

Sunday 13th

Made the dinner to "Family Favourites". Grandpa came for a short while. Made a start on my project on "Health & Hygiene". Mum & I went to church

& it was packed. It was Harvest Thanksgiving, and the church was full of scaffolding as it is being redecorated. Bed: 10.40 p.m.

Monday 14th
Was quite a good day at Tech. Stayed fine all day. Heard about Brenda's bike being pinched. Bed: 10.20 p.m.

Tuesday 15th
Had a good day. Was supposed to go to Auction last lesson but when we got to town we couldn't find Mr. Edwards. Helped Mum with shopping at night. Bed: 10.50 p.m.

Wednesday 16th
Was a cold day. The Olympics started on Saturday in Mexico & Dad & Ian have been watching them. Bed: 10.45 p.m.

Thursday 17th
It was Vicky's birthday & I bought her a box of chocs. Kept fine all day. Bed: 10.45 p.m.

Friday 18th
Had 3 hours of typing (uuk!). Was dull & cold all day. Washed hair & had bath at night. Bed: 11.15 p.m.

Saturday 19th
Was depressed a lot in the morning. In the afternoon helped to clean car & took Mum to hairdressers. At night did my homework & watched the thriller film called "Footsteps in the Fog". Mum & Dad went to Post Office dance to Acker Bilk. Bed: 1.5 a.m.

Sunday 20th
Did a bit of cooking after getting up late. Did not do much else except do a bit of my project & watch telly. Bed: 10.35 p.m.

Monday 21st
Had quite a good day. Was quite mild. Heard about power cut in Peterborough last night when our lights just dipped. Ian has got the whole week off for half term. Dad had a rotten cold. Bed: 10.55 p.m.

Tuesday 22nd
Had quite a good day at Tech. in the lessons. Was very foggy in morning. Had my hair trimmed at night & helped mum with the shopping. Bed: 10.45 p.m.

Wednesday 23rd
Was an o.k. day at Tech but not for making friends. Was only a little bit foggy. Bed: 10.50 p.m.

Thursday 24th
Wasn't a bad day. Saw a childbirth film in Domestic Science. Did not have to babysit after all. Bed: 10.45 p.m.

Friday 25th
Wasn't too bad at Tech apart from typing. Saw Mr. McIntyre the Principal for the first time. Mum & Dad went for a dancing lesson at night. Washed hair, had a bath & watched telly. Bed: 11.15 p.m.

Saturday 26th
Spent most of day in bed 'cos didn't feel too well with my stomach ache. At night did my homework & tidied my bedroom. Bed: 12.30 a.m.

Sunday 27th
Did a few house jobs. Grandpa came. Saw absolutely gorgeous film in afternoon that I had seen before called "Seventh Heaven" with James Stewart. Bed: 10.40 p.m.

Monday 28th
Had quite a good day at Tech. It rained nearly all day. Bed: 10.35 p.m.

Tuesday 29th
Had a good day at Tech. Did a lot of revising at night for commerce test. Bed: 10.30 p.m.

Wednesday 30th
Had commerce test & it was disastrous for some. Nothing special happened. Bed: 10.30 p.m.

Thursday 31st *HALLOWEEN!* 🦇
Didn't do games 'cos it was wet through pouring all morning. Missed the bus so I walked all the way home. [3 miles] Bed: 10.20 p.m.

November

Friday 1st
Was okay day. Rained quite a lot at dinner time & at night. Washed hair & had a bath. Got a bit depressed. Bed: 11.25 p.m

Saturday 2nd

Rained & was windy all day. News of floods in some places. Mum was at work in morning, I went to town. At night I went babysitting while Mum, Dad & Ian went to a firework display on the Old Showground. Waited for Bill [McFarlane] & *Smudge* [? Smith] *at night with the Green Shield stamp gifts but they did not turn up. Bed: 12.15 a.m.*

Sunday 3rd

Was a cold day. Did my homework & sewed up the hem on my skirt. My hair looked nice despite the rough weather yesterday. At night Bill from Cambridge came but Dad had gone to the pictures. Bed: 10.55 p.m.

Monday 4th

Had a good day. Was very cold. Had quite a lot of homework at night. Dad had to bath Topsy because she didn't smell very sweet. Bed: 10.50 p.m.

Tuesday 5th

It is Guy Fawkes day already. It was a cold day again with frost. My typing went all wrong. Ian had 3 rockets to set off. Bed: 11.00 p.m.

Wednesday 6th

Stayed dull & cold all day. I had two jumpers on. My hair still looked nice even though it was the middle of the week. Herman of the Hermits got married. Bed: 10.45 p.m.

Thursday 7th

Didn't have games 'cos it was wet so typed a letter to Sue in Wigan. [Penfriend Susan Forster, Four Winds, 158 Tower Hill, Upholland, Nr. Wigan, Lancs]. *Nothing special happened. Bed: 10.25 p.m.*

Friday 8th

At night washed my hair & had a bath. Mum & Dad went to dancing lessons while I stayed with Ian & watched telly. Bed: 11.20 p.m.

Saturday 9th

Was cold again. Went to town in morning, cleaned my bedroom in the afternoon. At night Mum & Dad went to the Posh Club so I watched telly & did my project. Bed: 12.30 a.m.

Sunday 10th

Didn't wake up till about dinner time. Took dog for a walk and phoned Brenda. It was a bit foggy. Watched telly for rest of day. Saw film "My Cousin Rachel" again. At night I babysat for Canhams. Bed: 11.30 p.m.

Monday 11th

Drizzled a bit in the morning. It was hard concentration in typing. Took sandwiches for dinner. Nothing special happened. Bed: 10.40 p.m.

Tuesday 12th

Was cold again. Typing wasn't too bad. Nothing special happened. Bed: 10.30 p.m.

Wednesday 13th

At night baked a cake for the Autumn Fair. Watched "Cathy Come Home" on the telly but it wasn't all that spectacular. Bed: 11.5 p.m.

Thursday 14th

Was a bit windy. Phoned up at Tech. about dance at Wirrina. At night did a lot of homework & watched "Miss World" on telly. Miss Australia won. Bed: 11.5 p.m.

Friday 15th

Was a very cold day. Nothing much happened. Washed hair & had bath at night. Bed: 10.45 p.m.

Saturday 16th

Was very cold again. We all went to town in morning & bought an electric fire. At night I went to a dance at the Wirrina. I didn't enjoy myself very much though. Bed: 1.50 p.m.

Sunday 17th

Was drizzling all day. Made the Christmas cake. At night I went with Dad & Ian for a quick visit to Piccavers for some potatoes. Bed: 10.40 p.m.

Monday 18th

Drizzled all day. Nothing special happened. Bed: 11.00 p.m.

Tuesday 19th

Was a dull cold day. Nothing special happened. Bed: 10.20 p.m.

Wednesday 20th

Was a bit warmer today. Realized it is getting so near Christmas. Forgot my dinner so had to buy some sandwiches. Came to a conclusion that Tech isn't bad at all now. Bed: 10.45 p.m.

Thursday 21st
Had quite an enjoyable day. At night had a bit of stomach ache. Now I've just got to con somebody into going to the Wirrina with me on Sat. Bed: 10.00 p.m.

Friday 22nd
Everybody did not seem to be happy but I was. It was my first time as receptionist but nobody came in. Washed hair & had a bath at night. Mum & Dad went to dance lesson. Bed: 11.10 p.m.

Saturday 23rd
Had headache. Went up town late in the afternoon. It was very crowded there. When I got home Mr. & Mrs. Bedford were just leaving. At night did my homework. Bed: 12.5 a.m.

Sunday 24th
Took dog for walk & rang Brenda. Did my cake with marzipan. Watched film called "Letter from an unknown Woman". Did a bit of homework & taped "Pick of the Pops". Bed: 11.15 p.m.
P.S. Saw the Royal Variety Performance.

Monday 25th
Was O.K. at Tech. Nothing special happened. Went to bed early 'cos of dance tomorrow night. Bed: 10.50 p.m.

Tuesday 26th
Drizzled all day. Went to this great dance at night at the Wirrina. Bed: 11.35 p.m.

Wednesday 27th
Drizzled and rained all day again. Made Grandma a birthday cake & did part of my homework. Bed: 10.40 p.m.

Thursday 28th
Was a very foggy day. Got let out of Tech. at 3 p.m. Went with Mum to a lingerie party at night & ordered a petticoat. Bed: 10.45 p.m.

Friday 29th
Was Grandma's birthday & Dad took over the cake I had made. At night Mum & Dad went to the Fireman's Ball. Bed: 10.45 p.m.

Saturday 30th

Went to town with Dad & Ian. At night Bill & Smudge came but I went to Wirrina, they brought my lamp. It was quite good at the dance. Was a bit disappointed in the beginning though. Bed: 12.45 a.m.

December

Sunday 1st

Iced my Christmas cake. Did a bit of homework & watched the film. Mum & Dad went to see Mr. & Mrs. Hazel & Liz & Dave. Bed: 10.10 p.m.

Monday 2nd

Started off the day OK. Was a bit foggy but it cleared. Bed: 9.55 p.m.

Tuesday 3rd

Tech wasn't too good. Had quite a good time at the dance. Bed: 11.40 p.m.

Wednesday 4th

Felt a bit sick but Brenda was feeling ill. Got a bit too hungry. Changed typewriters from my brand new Imperial 80 to a 70. Liked the 70 better because it was easier. Bed: 10.25 p.m.

Thursday 5th

Felt a bit better today. Wasn't bad at Tech. at all. Didn't have hockey so typed a letter. Bed: 10.35 p.m.

Friday 6th

Wasn't all that good at Tech. At night washed my hair, had a bath & then went babysitting. Bed: 12.00 a.m.

Saturday 7th

Didn't do much in the day. At night went to the Wirrina but it wasn't ever so good. Bed: 12.15 a.m.

Sunday 8th

Iced the trimmings on my cake & it was OK. Finished off my health project. Brenda came at night & I was glad. Bed: 10.20 p.m.

Monday 9th

Had a good day at Tech. 'cos made my mind up to have one. Brenda, Joy & I just walked to the shops at dinner time. Bed: 10.55 p.m.

Tuesday 10th

The day wasn't bad. Nothing special happened. It was cold. Bed: 10.20 p.m.

Wednesday 11th

Had quite a good day. Tried to make a few arrangements about the dance tomorrow. Nothing special happened. Bed: 9.30 p.m.

Thursday 12th

Took my things to Tech. & stayed with Brenda the night. Went to the Hotpoint dance. Bed: about 12.15 a.m.

Friday 13th

Didn't have a very good morning but afternoon was O.K. Came home & washed my hair & had a bath. Bed: 11.15 p.m.

Saturday 14th

Got a few of the Christmas trimmings up. It was the coldest day this winter with frost everywhere. It was below freezing. Mum & Dad went to Posh Club. Bed: 12.35 a.m.

Sunday 15th

Mum was sick in bed in the morning. In the late afternoon we went down to the Green's at Holbeach Drove to take present. Had tea there. Got a sore throat. Bed: 10.40 p.m.

Monday 16th

Still had a sore throat but it went. Got quite a few Christmas cards, after the weekend. Was a cold day but it rained. Ian stayed at home 'cos he felt sick. Bed: 10.5 p.m.

Tuesday 17th

My cold wasn't bad at all. It rained quite a lot in the day. Glad I went to the dance but didn't work out very good. Bed: 11.20 p.m.

Wednesday 18th

Had quite a good day at Tech. Went to Library for the first time with Brenda in the dinner hour. At night missed 2 buses 'cos of Christmas shoppers. Mr. Canham took Julia & I to Eye. Felt warm all day. Did a lot at night towards Christmas. Bed: 10.25 p.m.

Thursday 19th

Was quite a good day at Tech., but Typing got a bit tiring and monotonous. At night Mum's friend Patricia came with the petticoats. Bed: 10.15 p.m.

Friday 20th

Had quite a good time on the last day at Tech. Got all my Christmas presents. Got a ticket for the Tech. dance. Brenda had a lot to tell me. Washed my hair & had a bath at night. Bed: 10.00 p.m.

Saturday 21st *Didn't do much all day. At night went to Tech. dance with Barbara. It was good but I had a bad headache. Bed: 12.50 a.m.*

Sunday 22nd

Had to take tablets to get rid of my headache in morning. Took dog for walk & phoned Brenda. Did a little housework. In evening the Cranswicks came for a short while just before tea. At night watched "Forsyte Saga" & the film. Bed: 11.40 p.m.

Monday 23rd

Got up quite late. Dad, Ian & I went to Grandma's, town & Auntie Sheila's. It was hectic in town & I didn't get half the things I wanted. Got home late. Bed: 11.30 p.m.

Tuesday 24th

In the morning I delivered all Grandma's presents. In the afternoon I made some mince pies & cleared the house up a bit. At night we went to Auntie Freda's & then a quick visit to take presents to Jill & John but they had gone to Perkins Club. Bed: 11.20 p.m.

Wednesday 25th 🎅 🔔

Got up quite late. It didn't snow but drizzled. Grandma & Grandpa came for the day. Had our meals, watched telly & played one game of cards. Kept cheerful. Saw good funny film at night called "Some like it hot". Bed: 12.45 p.m.

Thursday 26th

Got up late. Mr. & Mrs. Bedford came after breakfast (dinner time) & stayed till late afternoon. Grandma & Grandpa came in for minute on their way to Aunt Violet's. At night watched telly & listened to my wireless. Finished book "Portrait of Margarita". Ate a lot of chocolate again & felt sick. Bed: 12.45 a.m.

Friday 27th

Felt lazy & got a bit bored. It was freezing outside but didn't snow. At night we went to the Bedfords, Ian stayed at home. Got a bit depressed. Bed: 11.45 p.m.

Saturday 28th

Went up town with Mum, Dad & Ian & got me a white jumper. Washed my hair & had a bath in the afternoon. Mum & Dad went to Post Office dance at Tech. Phoned Brenda. Bed: 1.15 p.m. P.S. Snow lay on the ground all day.

Sunday 29th

Got up at midday. Cleaned my bedroom & was very bored afterwards. It snowed finely through the day. Mum & I went to church. Saw a film at night about Marie Curie. Bed: 11.15 p.m.

Monday 30th

It didn't snow anymore but snow still lay on the ground. Was very bored through the day & was cold. Rang Brenda at night & confirmed our plans about Thursday. Bed: 11.30 p.m.

Tuesday 31st *Made myself busy & occupied myself in the day. The snow was partly melting but no fresh falls. Mum & Dad went to buffet & dance at Tech. College. Saw the new year in by watching the telly & playing Monopoly. The telly programmes were good. Bed: 2.40 a.m.*

NINE TIMES OUT OF TEN

Nine times out of ten life seems to work out for the best.
Nine times out of ten you find that if you let things rest -
Providence will sort them out without your helping hand -
Not perhaps in exactly the way you had planned - but in a wiser way and
from a broader point of view. So do not try to force events or push your own
plans though. Cease to worry. Trust and pray. Though things look black as
night - Nine times out of ten you find that everything comes right.

PATIENCE STRONG.

"For when the One Great Scorer comes
To write against your name
He marks - not that you won or lost -
But how you played the game."

Grantland Rice.

1969 The Lost Year

Unfortunately, out of the 50+ years I have kept a diary the one year missing is 1969. This disappeared a long time ago and probably because I moved 5 times in 5 years between 1974 and 1982 and yet, since that time I have lived in the same house for 34 years.

I have had to recall the major events of that year. I turned 16 in the January and was in my first and second year of a commercial course at Peterborough Technical College. I was busy at breaks and lunchtimes socialising throughout the corridors mixing with the boys which was a new concept for me. I know we liked to steer clear of the 'common room' as it stank of stale smoke. The refectory was used on occasions but the Principal of the college complained that girls wore their hair loose and it would trail in the food! We were always on diets and so for lunch we would usually eat a yoghurt in the cloakroom. Princess Alexandra was coming to open the new wing of the college and I was one of the chosen few to have tea with her. I was really stressed about this and didn't want to do it as I was worried I would do or say something wrong. Anyway, from what I remember it was fine, I talked mainly to a lady-in-waiting, and a girl called Linda from our course presented the bouquet of flowers.

My first boyfriend was from Scotland as the Scottish lads seemed more sensible and they were at the college on a 'sandwich' course each term in the engineering block. His name was Drew (Andrew) and he was rather sweet. I remember my first kiss, which I didn't like, sitting in the bay window of a pub. The next term I went out with another Scottish boy called Zander (Alexander) and I was becoming more accustomed to the kissing lark!

  I think I had two holidays in the summer. One in Cornwall and Devon with my parents and brother, the highlight was finding 'Jamaica Inn' as I was reading all the Daphne Du Maurier books. We towed a very small caravan and my dad was worried on every brow of a hill that the towing mechanism would snap and we would lose our portable holiday home!

The next holiday was with my friend Brenda, her father, stepmother Maura, and two half sisters Annette aged 2 and baby Caroline. We kept Annette entertained but also had time to ourselves to walk, sunbathe and play on the amusements and fun fair. We stayed in a flat in a house called 'The Pebbles' which is the photo on the front of this book, and I sent a postcard home to my parents.

So back to 'Tech' college for the start of the 2nd and final year of the course. This was the academic year that most of my friends would be turning 17 and my friend Vicky, from school and who was on the same commercial course as me, got engaged to Rob Chapman. I vaguely remember having a wild time (for me) at the party in Stamford where her future in-laws lived, at the back of their shoe and boot repairer's shop. Vicky was wearing a black maxi dress which I really wanted.

I was planning an escape for Christmas and hoping to spend the week with my second cousin Simon, his brother Andrew, Aunty Doris and Great Aunty Lil in Wales. I thought it was a good idea at the time but as the date approached I was becoming rather nervous as I didn't really know my Welsh relatives very well at all. Firstly I had to change coaches at Cheltenham and I was worried that I would not find the connection or even miss it. To make matters worse there was SNOW falling fast, the day I was set to travel! I remember being waved off at the coach station by Mum, Dad and Ian and putting on a brave face but was miserable and worried the whole way. Fortunately it all went smoothly but for the first few days I hardly ate anything and didn't sleep very well. My Aunt suggested I write a notelet to my parents to let them know I had arrived safely. I did this wishing I was back home as I missed them all, that is, until I met a friend of my cousin's, called Martyn……..!

Newport,
Mon.

Dear Mum, Dad and Ian,

Just a note to say that I arrived safely and on time. I didn't have any trouble changing at Cheltenham and the snow had all melted when we got outside of Peterborough. Everybody is well over here.

I'll probably write later on when I have more news to tell. Hope you have a happy Christmas.

Bye for now,
Love from
Sally xxx

Miscellaneous photographs which represent the era.

1966 probably Weymouth. Our typical caravan holidays and making friends with our neighbours.

I was one of the competition winners in Peterborough Advertiser's 'Junior Advertiser'. The competition was to write a piece on why you would like to visit America.

My parents' passport photos in 1967 when smiling was allowed.

PETERBOROUGH JOINT EDUCATION BOARD

THE JOHN MANSFIELD SECONDARY SCHOOL

Report for Term ending. 18th December 1964

Name Sally McDonald   Age 11 yrs. 10 mths.

Year 1st   Form 1A²   Average Age of Form 11 yrs 8 mths.

Number of Children in Form 34

Subject	Marks Possible	Marks Earned	Position in Form	Comments
Religious Instruction	100			
	100			Sally has produced some pleasing work
Literature	100	62	13	Good
Speech				'H' week
History	—	100	50	29	Satisfactory. H.P
Geography	—	100	63	16	Sally works well.
Mathematics Arithmetic				Sally works hard. After a poor
Algebra	150	101	30	start to the term she is now
Geometry				doing much better work
Science	—	100	70	2/19	Sally works well.
French	—	50	47	2	Very good progress. Sally has confidence and ability. J.D
Needlework	—	GRADE III		Quite good.
Housecraft	—			
Physical Education	GRADE III			Fair G.L.B
Art	—	GRADE III		Fair 87.
Crafts	—	GRADE I		Good neat work. J.D.
Music	—	GRADE I		Fairly satisfactory.
General Neatness	GRADE I			
Times Late	0			
Attendance to 11 Dec	126	124		

General Report : Sally has worked well this term. Although very quiet she is gradually gaining more confidence.

S.P.Malster.   Form Mistress

R.F. Newton   Head Mistress

My first school report at John Mansfield Secondary School for Girls.

Hodney Bridge over the railway, my bicycle route to school. In the background are the buckets of clay on an aerial ropeway from the Dogsthorpe Star Works to the Northam Brick Pits on the Crowland Road. Thiese have disappeared, along with the railway, and the bridge continues to go over the bypass road for Eye.

A reunion evening for John Mansfield School in 2007. Here I am with school friend Vicky and our form room lockers.

Also by Sally George

Sally's Diary. Leaving home in the 1970s. Peterborough-Cardiff-Birmingham.

Looking Back to the 1980s. Sally's Diary: Family Life in an East Yorkshire Town.

Blog:
theonlysallyg.wordpress.com

Lightning Source UK Ltd.
Milton Keynes UK
UKRC02n1025160517
301271UK00001B/2